Contents

	page
John Arden	v
Plot	ix
Commentary	xiii
Meanings	xiii
Characters	xvi
Origins	xxiii
Verbal and visual poetry	xxvii
Critical reception	xxxii
Further reading	xxxv
SERJEANT MUSGRAVE'S DANCE	
Introduction by John Arden	5
Act One	9
Act Two	38
Act Three	76
Notes	105

Mrs Hitchcock (*above*) and the three colliers (*below*) in the original 1959 production (*Photos: Snowdon*)

JOHN ARDEN

Serjeant Musgrave's Dance

An Un-historical Parable

With Commentary and Notes by
GLENDA LEEMING

METHUEN DRAMA

Methuen Student Edition

This Methuen Student Edition first published in 1982 by Methuen London Ltd
Reprinted 1985, 1986
Reprinted in 1992 by Methuen Drama
an imprint of Reed Consumer Books Ltd
Michelin House, 81 Fulham Road, London SW3 6RB
and Auckland, Melbourne, Singapore and Toronto

Reprinted 1993
Reissued with a new cover design 1994

Serjeant Musgrave's Dance first published in 1960 by Methuen & Co Ltd.
Reset and reprinted, 1966.

Printed and bound in Great Britain by
Cox & Wyman Ltd, Reading, Berkshire

ISBN 0 413 49260 5

Front cover photograph shows Ian Bannen as Serjeant Musgrave.
(photo: Snowdon)

Thanks are due to James Gibbs, Malcolm Page, Non Worrall, Stephen Wyatt and John Arden for their help and advice in the preparation for this edition.

John Arden

(*At John Arden's own suggestion, this chronology concentrates on the years up to* Armstrong's Last Goodnight *as being the period most likely to be of interest to readers of* Serjeant Musgrave's Dance. *Since 1965 (and occasionally before that) he has pursued a second career with Margaretta D'Arcy which runs partly parallel to his own solo work but is distinct from it. Further information about this can be found in Arden's book of essays,* To Present the Pretence, *Eyre Methuen, 1977, and in the chapter devoted to Arden and D'Arcy in Catherine Itzin's survey of political theatre in the British Isles since 1968,* Stages in the Revolution, *Eyre Methuen, 1980.*)

1930 John Arden born in Barnsley, Yorkshire. Spent a few years at a local Elementary School but at the beginning of the war was sent away from this industrial area in case there was bombing, to a boarding school. Later he went to the public school, Sedbergh. Although there was little professional theatre to be seen in the area, he acted in plays at school, was always interested in dramatic form, and began writing at about sixteen – mostly long historical plays.

1949-50 National Service as a lance-corporal in the Intelligence Corps of the Army.

1950-3 Went to King's College, Cambridge, to study architecture.

1953-5 Completed his architectural training at Edinburgh College of Art, where his first play, *All Fall Down,* was presented by a student cast (which included himself).

1955-7 Completed his qualifications by working for two years in an architect's office in London. Meanwhile, worked on *The Waters of Babylon* which was included in the short list of best entrants for *The Observer* playwriting competition. His radio play, *The Life of Man*, won a prize from the BBC North of England region. This prize drew him to the attention of George Devine, who had just taken over the

Royal Court Theatre, London, where he had staged Osborne's *Look Back in Anger* in May 1956. *The Waters of Babylon* was put on there, and when the Royal Court commissioned *Live Like Pigs,* Arden became a full time writer. He married Margaretta D'Arcy, an Irish actress.

1958 *When is a Door not a Door*? commissioned by the Central School of Drama, London, to give equal acting opportunities to the cast of students – so Arden gave it the theme of social equality – and *Live Like Pigs* finished and produced at the Royal Court.

1959 *Serjeant Musgrave's Dance* directed by Lindsay Anderson at the Royal Court. It was kept on in spite of mainly hostile reviews and loss of money, and made enough impact to become 'a modern classic'.

1959-60 Awarded *Encyclopaedia Britannica* prize and took up a year's playwriting fellowship at the University of Bristol, where he wrote *The Happy Haven* in collaboration with Margaretta D'Arcy for the University's small open-stage theatre. He won an *Evening Standard* award in 1960, and had his television play, *Soldier, Soldier,* produced. (This had been written before *Live Like Pigs* but Arden saw certain similarities between its plot, about a modern soldier arriving with ambiguous purpose in an unknown town, and *Serjeant Musgrave's Dance.*) Arden and D'Arcy wrote a Christmas play, *The Business of Good Government,* to be acted by the villagers of Brent Knoll in Somerset: the main character, an unhistorical King Herod, gets unwillingly involved, like Serjeant Musgrave, in a massacre of the innocents.

1961 *Soldier, Soldier* awarded the Trieste Festival prize. A second television play, *Wet Fish,* produced without Arden's participation.

1962 *Serjeant Musgrave's Dance* shown on BBC Television.

1963 *Ironhand,* Arden's translation and adaptation of Goethe's *Goetz von Berlichingen,* produced at the Bristol Old Vic, and although he considered it 'too far from the original, yet not far enough to be a work in its own right' he used it as a source later for *Armstrong's Last Goodnight* 'and a little for *Left-Handed Liberty*'. *The Workhouse Donkey,* a satirical comedy set in a modern northern town, performed by the National Theatre Company at the Chichester Festival Theatre. *Serjeant Musgrave's Dance* directed by

Peter Brook in French in Paris.

1964 Arden and D'Arcy collaborated on the first of several less conventionally structured plays, *Ars Longa, Vita Brevis*. Glasgow Citizens' Theatre put on *Armstrong's Last Goodnight*: inspired by Conor Cruise O'Brien's book about present-day Katanga, but set within the framework of the old Scottish Ballad of Johnny Armstrong, the language throughout is a deliberately archaic Scottish dialect.

1965 *Armstrong* produced in London by the National Theatre Company. Arden adapted a libretto of Beethoven's *Fidelio* and was commissioned to write *Left-Handed Liberty*, to commemorate the 750th anniversary of the signing of Magna Carta by King John. *Serjeant Musgrave's Dance* staged in a new production at the Royal Court with Iain Cuthbertson in the lead.

1966 American premiere of *Serjeant Musgrave's Dance*. *Friday's Hiding** staged at Lyceum Theatre, Edinburgh. *The Royal Pardon** staged at Beaford in Devon.

1968 *Squire Jonathan* staged at Ambiance Theatre Club, London. *The Hero Rises Up** staged at the Round House, London. *Harold Muggins is a Martyr** staged by CAST (Cartoon Archetypical Slogan Theatre) at Unity Theatre, London.

1970 *The Bagman, or, The Impromptu of Muswell Hill* broadcast on BBC Radio.

1972 *The Ballygombeen Bequest** staged on tour by 7:84 Theatre Company. *The Island of the Mighty** staged by the Royal Shakespeare Company at the Aldwych Theatre, London. A new version of *Serjeant Musgrave* by John McGrath, called *Serjeant Musgrave Dances On*, in which Musgrave became a paratroop sergeant coming back from the troubles in present-day Northern Ireland, was staged on tour by 7:84 Theatre Company.

1975 *The Non-Stop Connolly Show** staged in Dublin and given public readings in London.

1977 Arden's own selection of his essays 'on the theatre and its public' published under the title *To Present the Pretence*.

1978 *Pearl* broadcast on BBC Radio. *Vandaleur's Folly** staged on tour by 7:84 Theatre Company.

1980 Arden's two-part dramatisation of *Don Quixote* broadcast on BBC Radio. Arden wrote another radio play, *Garland for a Hoar Head*.

1981 The National Theatre, London, mounted a new production of *Serjeant Musgrave's Dance* with John Thaw in the lead, which was well received by critics and played to full houses. Arden worked throughout the year on a novel, *Silence Among the Weapons.*

* *Denotes a play collaboratively written by John Arden and Margaretta D'Arcy (see note on page v).*

Two sets from the original 1959 production. The churchyard (*above*) and the bar of the public house (*below*). (*Photos: Snowdon*)

Plot

Four deserters bring the body of a dead soldier back to his home town, a mining community in the grip of a coalstrike, and cut off by the winter snow. Their leader plans to hold the town at gun-point, while, in a public meeting, he presents the dead soldier's skeleton and brings people face to face with the truth about war. But things go wrong. One of the soldiers, Sparky, tries to run away with a barmaid called Annie, and is accidentally killed. At the climax of Musgrave's meeting, Annie produces Sparky's body. The meeting collapses, the snow thaws, the dragoons arrive, and one more of the deserters is killed. At the end of the play the town celebrates its escape, while the two remaining soldiers, Attercliffe and Musgrave himself, wait to be hanged.
(from *Arden – A Study of his Plays*, Albert Hunt, Eyre Methuen, 1974, p.58)

The plot of *Serjeant Musgrave's Dance* is one of gradually revealed purposes, with the action speeding up to a climax as these purposes meet with interruptions and opposition. The action takes place sometime between 1860 and 1880.

Act I Scene i: The opening scene is mysterious. It seems that the reason why a party of four soldiers is on its way to a coal-mining town in the north of England is not simply to seek recruits: Hurst's natural aggressiveness is increased by obvious but unexplained nervousness; and young Sparky's persistent chatter and singing is punctuated by odd remarks which alarm the others; even Attercliffe, the oldest and apparently the most confident of the three, is irritable and anxious. References to 'court martial', 'gallows' and 'bones' suggest that there is a dangerous secret here. The bargee, Joe Bludgeon, comes to take the soldiers to the town on his barge, and though his malicious talk is quelled by the authority of the last soldier to arrive, Serjeant Musgrave, the bargee's insolent final rhyme questions the Serjeant's gravity and authority.
Act I Scene ii: In the town, the people discuss their own troubles.

The Mayor owns the coal mines, and because of poor economic conditions he has decided to lower the miners' wages and dismiss some men. The miners ('colliers'), members of a Trades Union, having threatened to strike, the Mayor closes his mines so that no-one can work at all until they agree to his terms. Thus the representatives of law and order – the Mayor, the Parson and the Constable – are worried about the danger of violence from the resentful miners. They hope that the soldiers will provide a diversion and perhaps take away some of the idle men. Musgrave appears to cooperate with them, but again some underlying secret seems to motivate his enquiries about a dead fellow soldier from this town, Billy Hicks. Mrs. Hitchcock, the landlady of the public house where they are lodging, reveals that Billy was the father of Annie's now dead illegitimate baby: Annie helps in the bar, though the loss of Billy and the baby has disturbed her sanity.
Act I Scene iii: This scene is set in the churchyard. Having surveyed the town, the soldiers talk among themselves. We learn their true purpose: appalled by a night of violent reprisals for one soldier's death in a campaign overseas, they have come to convince people that the colonial war, and its use of men to repress other men by violence, is wrong. To bring this message they have stolen money and deserted, and this town was chosen because it was the home of Billy Hicks, whose death provoked the reprisals. Interrupting this talk, the colliers appear and threaten them, but Musgrave knows that their dislike of soldiers is not a real recognition of the evils of war and violence.

Act II Scene i: A scene of jollity in Mrs Hitchock's bar shows the soldiers acting out their roles as recruiters. Meanwhile Sparky tries to impress Annie, but she prefers the handsome Hurst and agrees to come to his bed that night, though Musgrave warns her not to distract his men from their duty.
Act II Scene ii: Walsh, the earnest collier and strike leader, tries to make his friends ashamed of being tempted into drunkenness and forgetting their struggle to win the strike; but in vain. Musgrave tries to engage Walsh's sympathy; also in vain. Afterwards the bargee suggests that the colliers should steal the soldiers' gun.
Act II Scene iii: Here things begin to go wrong for Musgrave. As the Serjeant settles in his bedroom and the others in the stable, Annie comes to Hurst, but he rejects her, being now preoccupied by Musgrave's ideas; and Attercliffe also refuses her, telling how

his own wife took a greengrocer for a lover, leaving him too embittered for love. At first Annie is too upset to respond to Sparky, but eventually they confide in each other, and Sparky decides that each has been hurt enough by senseless deaths, and that these can be better atoned for by living, not further suffering. During this talk, Musgrave's own anxieties break out in a nightmare. Hurst overhears Sparky planning to run away with Annie, and as they all struggle, Sparky is killed falling on a bayonet held by the peaceful Attercliffe. Musgrave hurries in to take charge of the crisis, but as they are hiding the body, another crisis arises: Bludgeon betrays the colliers who are following his own plan of stealing the soldiers' guns. Walsh is captured and his comrades chased off, then in order to win Walsh's confidence Musgrave hides him from the Constable. As a final blow, the Mayor arrives to say that the town is no longer cut off by snow and dragoons have been sent for. Musgrave announces that he will hold a recruiting meeting next morning – apparently to occupy and distract the town, but in fact because it is his last chance to act.

Act III Scene i: Most of this Act is taken up with the climactic recruiting meeting, introduced by the Mayor and Parson. First Musgrave demonstrates the frightening power of the automatic Gatling gun, then tells with mounting passion of the danger and duties of a soldier's life. At the peak of this speech the other large box is opened and a skeleton in a red tunic is hauled up to hang from the market cross. Musgrave threatens the crowd with the weapons and tells them how stupid and arbitrary was the violence that followed this corpse's death. Only after Walsh has expressed dislike of war and the army but no positive interest in opposing them does Musgrave reveal that the skeleton was Billy Hicks. The Serjeant then reasons that the five killings provoked by Hicks' death should be avenged by killing five times five townsfolk, as a lesson and a warning. Walsh is unconvinced, but though Attercliffe refuses to be involved in more violence, Hurst and the bargee are ready to shoot. Annie intervenes here in refusing to accept this kind of vengeance, and tells everyone of Sparky's death – this turns Walsh decisively against Musgrave. Hurst makes a final desperate attempt to fire into the crowd, but is overpowered by Attercliffe and Musgrave, and at the last moment the dragoons arrive just in time to shoot Hurst and arrest Musgrave and Attercliffe. The bargee changes sides again, and as the crowd takes advantage of the relaxed tension and free beer, only Walsh feels somehow cheated of a chance to act.

Act III Scene ii: The last short scene is something of a coda or epilogue. Mrs Hitchcock visits the prisoners, and Musgrave wonders where his plan went wrong. Attercliffe explains that he was wrong to fight violence with violence. Attercliffe and Mrs Hitchcock hope that they will be remembered and that their message itself, however imperfectly expressed, will spread.

Private Sparky and Annie in the 1965 revival (*Photo: Dominic*)

Commentary

Meanings

In spite of the immediate appeal of *Serjeant Musgrave's Dance*, with its strong characters and exciting plot, audiences and readers often find themselves confused at the end of the play. Where are our sympathies supposed to lie? Should we be sorry that Musgrave has failed to impress his message on the people? Or glad that he was prevented from massacring bewildered townsfolk? Is he responsible for Sparky's death? What exactly went wrong with the plan and was it Musgrave's fault? As Arden says in his author's preface (p. 7) 'the fact that the sympathies of the play are clearly with him in his original horror, and then turn against him and his intended remedy, seems to have bewildered many people'. This was intentional:

> I have grave objections to being presented with a character on the stage whom you know to be the author's mouthpiece . . . The result is that it all becomes predictable. I cannot see why a social play should not be so designed that we may find ourselves understanding the person's problems, but not necessarily approving his reactions to them. ('Building the Play', *Encore* no. 32, 1961, p.30)

The audience is *not* supposed to identify with Musgrave, and in the preface Arden recommends a 'study of the women and of Private Attercliffe' (p. 7) to clarify the play. Attercliffe, in the first place, is a pacifist, so one of his functions is to express the wrongness of the violence and brutality that is necessarily part of military action. We see how horrified he is at Sparky's death and how appalled at Musgrave's proposal to shoot twenty-five townspeople. So far his criticism is clear: killing is bad no matter what the circumstances. If Musgrave's plan involves killing, then it is no better than the wars they are trying to testify against.

Attercliffe and Musgrave have apparently been satisfied with army duty as long as it seemed reasonable and necessary – kill the enemy because he is dangerous or may kill you; as Musgrave says 'I called Death honest, killing by the book' (p.37). What changed their minds was the one incident in which, as a reprisal for the shooting of Billy Hicks, many of the colonial civilians were injured and five killed. But these victims were not guilty of anything in particular; they were killed and injured at random and arbitrarily – a fact that made Musgrave and Hurst question the rightness of their paid killings, and brought home to Attercliffe the horror of these undeserved deaths. But in eventually deciding to shoot twenty-five townspeople 'as an example', Musgrave is acting just as arbitrarily as the army authorities.

Attercliffe makes this point explicitly in the last scene. Violence cannot be stopped by more violence. 'To end it by its own rules: no bloody good' (p.102). In other words, what the army does in killing the enemy population without regard for feeling, human rights or justice, is echoed in Musgrave's rigid, inexorable plan which equally disregards the feelings and rights of his companions and the townsfolk.

This is why Sparky gets killed. His final personal decision is to protest against his friend Billy Hick's death by running away to a civilian life, but the harsh, inhuman system Musgrave is still working by does not allow for disagreement; Sparky *must* do exactly as the system demands, regardless of his own feelings and rights, or else force will be used to make him conform – in this case, with fatal results. 'He was killed by pure accident!' says Musgrave furiously (p. 101), but such accidents are to be blamed on the rigid system which insists 'Obey, or suffer', and permits no compromise. It may seem odd that this significant violent death takes place at the hands of the pacifist Attercliffe, who personally is the least aggressive of the soldiers. Yet, as when he first joined the army, in siding with Musgrave he has got involved with a violent system. Attercliffe is almost a personification in himself of the basic error of Musgrave's plan: his intentions and wishes are good, but the system he follows makes him act without humanity, contrary to his intentions.

Serjeant Musgrave cannot understand this. His whole plan has been unrealistically simple: he has failed to take account of the feelings and rights of others – they are 'not material'. He asks, 'What made it break down', and Mrs Hitchcock replies, 'Ah, there's the moral of it. You ask our Annie' (p. 101). Both she and Annie are significant in pointing this moral, and they are significant because to Musgrave they are *insignificant* – he ignores them. Or, at most, he considers them a danger: 'there's work is for women and there's work is for men: and let the two get mixed, you've anarchy', which to him means interruption of his straightforward plan. If, he says, 'you come to us with what you call your life or love', but which he calls 'indulgence', then, again, 'there's anarchy' (p.51). Life and love are not important to Musgrave, just as the military system does not value them. Annie brings this out when she intervenes in the climactic market place scene. Her sad story reminds us that the dead Billy Hicks whom she mourns is not just an army statistic, but the ending of life and love for a real human being. Then she shows the bayonet-pierced tunic in which Sparky died. What right, the colliers naturally wonder, have men to talk of stopping systematic military violence when they keep order by violence among themselves?

Mrs Hitchcock pours scorn on Musgrave's simple viewpoint, explaining 'here we are, and we'd got life and love. Then *you* came in and you did your scribbling where nobody asked you. Aye, it's arsy-versy to what you said, but it's still an anarchy, isn't it?' (p.102). He has disregarded the different problems of the town – as Mrs Hitchcock tells him, '*you* brought in a different war' (p.102) – in that his message is more abstract, and his decision to kill more arbitrary and unproductive. In fact Musgrave has almost convinced the earnest collier Walsh, one of the few to grasp what the soldiers are trying to say; but Walsh too notes Mrs Hitchock's point about a 'different' war: the colliers shooting their bosses would have been for an obvious reason. 'But that's one thing, y'see, and this is another – ent it' (p.92). Walsh and his friends are involved in a personal, direct struggle for their livelihoods, with obvious reasons for hating their enemies. Musgrave would be killing for the sake of an abstraction, as a warning to the world generally – just as in the army reprisal incident. Yet it is not true that Walsh and the others are wholly selfish and untouched by Musgrave's idealism, however dangerously expressed, although they fail to support him. Arden says, 'Accusations of nihilism seem to derive from the scene where the Colliers turn away from Musgrave and join in the general dance around the beer barrel' (p.7). Critics see this as nihilism because they feel Arden must be implying that no-one ever cares enough to act, that everyone gives in to greater pressures, or to circumstances, or to self-interest, so that everything will always stay the same. However, he is merely showing that 'an unwillingness to dwell upon unpleasant situations that do not immediately concern us is a general human trait, and recognition of it need imply neither cynicism nor despair' (p.7), and is not drawing a universal rule from this particular behaviour. Indeed, against this we have the final words of Mrs Hitchcock, 'Those men are hungry, so they've got no time for *you.* One day they'll be full though, and the Dragoons'll be gone, and then they'll remember' (p.102); and Attercliffe's final, hopeful question: 'D'you reckon we can start an orchard?' (p.104). So the last impression we are left with is a guarded hope that things may after all change.

Characters

It might seem that the characters in this play tend to 'stand for' abstract qualities, such as 'pacificism' or 'life and love', as discussed above – but a viewing or reading should soon show that this does not mean that the characters are over-simplified. They have many qualities that make them convincing and 'realistic', in the sense that they are as complex and unpredictable, though consistent, as the people we meet in the real world. And this is important to the over-all message of the play: Arden, as we have seen, stresses the complexity of life – as opposed to Musgrave's mistaken over-simplification – so naturally the characters must show complexity too.

The preface to the play introduces the characters in three main groups – the soldiers, the women and the townsmen. The soldiers are differentiated according to a range of masculine traits – the old, weary, seen-it-all-before Attercliffe, the cynical, violent Hurst, the cheerful, innocent young Sparky, and of course Serjeant Musgrave, the aloof, slightly mysterious figure of power and authority. In any military story, from the *Iliad* through the *Three Musketeers* to P.C. Wren's French Foreign Legion novels, two or more of these types will appear among the nucleus of main characters, and all four figures are used by modern dramatists R.C. Sherriff in *Journey's End* and Willis Hall in *The Long and the Short and the Tall.* Similarly, Mrs Hitchoock and Annie are a typical pair of contrasting female characters – the wise, older woman, a mother or motherly, and the young woman, either deserted and betrayed, or the whore with a heart of gold – both, in Annie's case. The point is that Arden is using figures that, like ballads, have strong popular traditions behind them and a strong popular appeal, but is fleshing out these figures into the complex individuals that his particular story needs. He began in fact with the soldiers' basic roles, and gradually built them up into more rounded personalities:

> I started off calling them 'One Soldier', 'Two Soldier', and 'Three Soldier', wrote a few scenes, decided they were developing certain characteristics of their own, went back and renamed them 'The Joking Soldier', 'The Surly Soldier', and 'The Grey-haired Soldier'. I finished the play and then when we went into rehearsal decided they had better have names – this was really Lindsay Anderson's idea. He maintained that if you call a character 'The Surly Soldier', it is going to make an actor think he has got to be surly all the way through. It was not until they had names that the soldiers really came alive as people. (*Encore* no. 32, 1961, pp.38-9)

The townsmen however are deliberately less developed as individuals.

> Of course people will say that the mayor and parson and the policeman in *Musgrave* are cardboard figures. Well, that's because they are engaged in a situation where only their public personalities are displayed, and I think that in the expression of their public personalities I have not caricatured them. It is caricature by omission rather than by exaggeration – I could envisage another play in which those three people appear without the coal strike and without the eruption of the soldiers. And they would be rounded figures. (*Tulane Drama Review*, 1966)

And of the colliers only Walsh, who starts out as 'the Earnest Collier', attains a name, his friends retaining type names to show that their main importance is as a group, as representatives of the large body of miners in the town. And the strange character, hunchbacked Joe Bludgeon, is addressed by his name, and indeed stresses his own name frequently, but is always labelled 'Bargee' in the stage directions – not a label that carries any particular quality or status with it, as does 'Mayor' or 'Slow Collier'. The Bargee's character is ambiguous, usually malevolent, and not, perhaps, to be pinned down by a name or label.

This is certainly the case with the soldiers: there is obviously much more to **Attercliffe**, for instance, than can be conveyed by the label 'Grey-haired Soldier'. He is, as the preface puts it, 'grey-haired, melancholy, a little embittered' (p.6) and from the first scene shows the authority his age gives him over the younger soldiers – 'keep watching . . . Steady, boy' (p.10). As we learn of Musgrave's purpose in Act I scene ii, Attercliffe stands up with great conviction for his own pacifist viewpoint: 'All wars, Serjeant Musgrave. They've got to turn against all wars . . . I've got a new life. There was one night's work, and I said: no more killing' (p.36). This is an almost religious dedication to this beliefs, yet in the stable scene his cynicism dominates, as he rejects Annie with 'Good strong girly with a heart like a horsecollar, open it up and let 'em all in. And it still wouldn't do no good' (p.60). And this embittered feeling partly derives from his individual history: his wife has gone off with a greengrocer who 'sold good green apples and he fed the people and he fed my wife' (p.61). Her rejection of himself and his soldiering, identified with 'Blood, y'see: killing' (p.51), has been another and personal buried motive for his conversion to pacifism. At the same time, his wife's implied dislike of blood and killing has made him feel self-disgust from his association with it – 'so now I'm a dirty old bastard in a red coat and blue breeches and that's all about it' (p.61). And contrasting with both his dedication to a good cause and his grim melancholy is his emotional, almost hysterical reaction to the violent impulses in other people. In the pub in Act II scene i he is 'trembling all over' when a fight breaks out and afterwards says, in sentences broken by strong feeling 'He was going to, Serjeant. He would have, he'd have killed him. It's always here. Kill him. Kill.' (p.47).

It is useful to compare Attercliffe with **Serjeant Musgrave** himself, who is also grave, responsible and dedicated to his purpose; as we have seen, Musgrave's fault is to ignore too many of the aspects of complex human existence that make people behave illogically. This narrowness of vision comes out in a difference of opinion with Attercliffe:

MUSGRAVE. . . . we've had to leave behind us a colonial war that is a war of sin and unjust blood.
ATTERCLIFFE (*sharply*). All wars is sin, serjeant . . .
MUSGRAVE (*impatient*). I'm not discussing that. Single purpose at a single time: your generalities aren't material: this is particular . . . (p.33)

Typically, Musgrave is leaving out too much, just as he leaves out the human consequences of the military system, such as the malformation and death of Annie's baby, either directly or symbolically connected with its father's death in the war, 'About the time they called him dead' (p.27), as Mrs Hitchcock says. Musgrave replies characteristically 'It's not material . . . Dead men and dead children should bide where they're put and not be rose up to the thoughts of the living. It's bad for discipline'. Ironically, it is Musgrave who hauls up the skeleton of dead Billy, and then finds he can't leave out the associated consequences. But Musgrave's vision of what is and is not important is essential to his character – he sees things in black and white, all or nothing. The 'dance' of the title is a metaphor for his vision, his understanding of the world: to him, life is, or should be, an orderly clear pattern showing God's will. The colonial war has departed from this orderliness by killing innocent people 'as an example' instead of for a good reason, and so the war must be condemned and stopped so that the world can return to God's logical, orderly will. Mostly, Musgrave has great confidence in his own vision of order, of right and wrong, 'as I understand Logic and Logic to me is the mechanism of God' (p.91), but even he, whose character seems to represent unity and fixity, has moments of doubt. In Act I scene iii he prays

> keep my mind clear so I can weigh Judgement against the Mercy and Judgement against the Blood, and make this Dance as terrible as You have put it into my brain. (p.37)

And during the stable scene Musgrave alone in his room has a nightmare, shouting loud enough to summon Mrs Hitchcock; his dream passes from 'Fire, fire', to the colonial massacre that has sent them all here, and ends with a count-down in which he is 'timing the end of the world'. This shows that, confident and peremptory though he may appear, the depths of this mind hide fears and doubts that he is having to repress, and that trouble him deeply once his guard is lowered by sleep. He says to Mrs Hitchcock

> The end of the world? You'll tell me it's not material, but if you could come to it, in control; I mean, numbers and order like so many ranks this side, so many that, properly dressed, steadiness on parade, so that whether you knew you was right, or you knew you was wrong – you'd know it and you'd stand. (p.65)

Could it be that Musgrave's insistence on clarity, order and control is his defence against a hidden fear – whether of death, or what comes after death, or simply of being caught unprepared? The strong serjeant is weak in his fear of the unknown.

Hurst shows similar signs of uneasiness, of a sense of being somehow threatened, so that he needs to be always on the defensive. This is why he rejects Annie in the stable scene, saying 'You want me to lose my life inside of you –' (p.59). Beyond the primitive idea that sleeping with a woman will weaken his strength, Hurst is afraid to let any feeling of kindness, gentleness or love interfere with the hard, aggressive attitude he needs to carry out the dangerous plan. Annie notices how like the serjeant he is in this singlemindedness – 'they *have* found him a brother' (p.59). His original motives are imperfectly expressed because he is 'browbeaten into incoherence' (p.30) but it seems that he particularly resents, as Musgrave does, being used by the army to do various things such as unnecessary killings, with all the immediate blood and guilt, for unknown or unsatisfactory reasons. Unlike Attercliffe, he is not opposed to killing in itself – he has evidently killed a personal enemy, 'a murdered officer', for what Musgrave allows to be a 'good reason' (p.29) – and there is even some fascination with violent methods in his outburst 'It's time we did our *own* killing' (p.36). Thus his violence in the market place, for all its justification 'You hurt them hard and they'll not hurt you again' (p.94), is tainted by his reckless eagerness to expend human lives – there is none of Musgrave's reluctance, and we can see in Hurst just how the enforcement of ideas by violence can accelerate into a general bloodbath.

It is a poignant feature of the play that **Sparky**, the most harmless and the least committed to the plan, is the first victim of that plan. Arden's initial description of him as 'easily led, easily driven, inclined to hide from himself behind a screen of silly stories and irritating clownishness' (p.6) tallies with Mrs Hitchcock's comment 'he was only a young lad, for gracious goodness Christ, he'd a voice like a sawmill' (p.101). He is quite happy to be distracted by Annie from his duty, and it is he who embraces and comforts her when the other two turn away. Of the soldiers, then, he is the one with life and love. Even his motives for following Musgrave are emotional and personal, as the closest friend of the dead Billy Hicks – 'Billy's dead. He wor my mucker, back end of the rear rank. He wor killed dead' (p.34); yet he has doubts about the point of 'paying for' Billy's death: 'I didn't want to pay for him – what had I to care for a colonial war?' The difference between his personal feeling, and the abstract position of the others comes over in his accusation of Hurst 'You didn't even know him when he lived, you weren't in his squad, what do *you* care that he's dead?' (p.35). And he suggests a convincing alternative to the fighting-violence-with-violence plan in his proposal to Annie 'suppose I paid for yours, why, maybe you could pay for mine' (p.63) meaning that each would not pay by further destroying, but by comforting each other: 'All it would be, is: *you* live and *I* live – we don't need his duty, we don't need his Word' (p.63).

Of course this ignores the wider problem of how to convince the rest of the world that this is better than systematic violence, but it is not quite the same as mere escapism; it is not the same as Walsh's turning away helplessly into the dance at the end, for Sparky is offering a positive suggestion here, a way of life in which caring for others solves problems, rather than force or Musgrave's inflexible, harsh rules.

If Sparky, the 'easily-led' young soldier, surprises us by producing from his affectionate nature a vision to set against Musgrave's, then **Annie**, as personifying 'life and love', is equally unexpected. A simple personification of these qualities would surely be happier, more beautiful, more good-tempered than Annie, who is unhappy, the mother of a dead child, and at the least mentally disturbed by successive bereavements; as Arden says 'Her emotional confusion expresses itself in a deliberately enigmatic style of speech and behaviour. Her voice is harsh' (p.7). Yet far from being 'daft' she can be very perceptive in her 'deliberately enigmatic' way; as in the verse she applies to Musgrave:

> The North Wind in a pair of millstones
> Was your father and your mother
> They got you in a cold grinding.
> God help us all if they get you a brother. (p.26)

His hardness and coldness have obviously impressed her already, and the danger accompanying them: the impression is confirmed by Musgrave himself 'She talks a kind of truth, that lassie' (p.26). She is associated with verse and song-ballads, but there is all the more pathos in the fact that she is not the conventional pretty maid of ballad story, but 'gay and greasy . . . big . . . and . . . bonny' (p.44) with a dirty face and a sooty neck; a 'whoor-to-the-soldiers' who can be tender and hurt at being rejected.

Less involved with the soldiers is **Mrs Hitchcock**, so that she remains more of a background figure until the last scene. For her, Arden's description is 'She is clearly a woman of deep sympathies and intelligence, which she disguises with the normal north-country sombre pessimism' (p.7). Her pessimism comes out in her concern with her own trade and her willingness to trust Musgrave, which is less trustfulness than fatalism: 'I've got to trust you, haven't I?' (p.70). She is both realistic, and ready to enjoy life if she can – the opposite of Attercliffe's self-denying cynicism. Her steady use of her own stock-in-trade of drinks – she is drinking tea with brandy in it in Act II scene i, she has hot grog at night 'for me bad back' (p.65) and port and lemon in the morning 'like it settles me stummick for the day' (p.101) – does not mean that she thinks only of her own indulgences. A comfortable and comforting woman, she tends the serjeant in his nightmare, just as she cares for Annie after Sparky's death. In the last scene her explanations about the soldiers' forced and forceful interference in the town underline Musgrave's indifference to everyone else's feelings and rights – to Mrs Hitchcock, as we have seen her in action, it is evidently essential that such feelings are considered.

The remaining characters, except for Walsh and the Bargee, are not on the whole as complex as those discussed above. The **Mayor, Parson** and **Constable** are those who have power to ensure that general difficulties – such as economic problems – will weigh more heavily on the powerless than on themselves. They are also the people who, as Musgrave and Hurst realise, are responsible for enabling unnecessary wars to continue (by promoting the recruitment of men to the army, by approving of the ethos of glory and accepting that their taxes go to support war, etc.). As representatives of the class in power, they have fairly simple, uncomplicated characteristics, such as the matter-of-fact, direct, bossy manner of the Mayor. He seems less enclosed in his public persona than the others: he reacts quickly to Musgrave's remarks, relates his own problems to a wider economic situation (falling prices, transport difficulties) and his local dialect shows him to have risen from a lower stratum of society, probably by his own efforts, rather than being born to education and privilege like the Parson.

Arden wanted privilege to be the important factor in the Parson's character: 'He must have the accent and manners of a balked aristocrat rather than a stage-clergyman' (p.6); he says nothing perceptive, intelligent or original, and his language is not only that of ready-made clichés, but *boring* clichés – 'our great country', 'petty differences', 'brave flag', 'manly spirit' (p.79). These clichés tend to hide any individuality the Parson may have. And the Constable is so much a cliché in action that he *does* seem exaggerated rather than briefly portrayed: like a pantomime policeman he bullies the colliers when he can, but is cowardly when threatened; Arden gets more broad humour from the gap between his supposed role of guardian of the law and the timid reality than from the Parson's hypocrisy.

Walsh, though embittered and beaten at the end, has a complex and ambivalent attitude towards right, wrong and the use of violence. It is interesting that Arden does not, as he might have done, make Walsh the spokesman of an acceptable political reformation. This would simplify the whole play by showing where Musgrave was wrong, – but simplification is not what Arden is after. Yet his objections to Musgrave's message – 'But that's one thing, y'see, and this is another' – makes an intelligent distinction; his grasp of wider issues gives substance to Mrs Hitchcock's hope that later Musgrave's message will take effect.

Finally, **the Bargee** (Joe Bludgeon) is a kind of mouthpiece for everything that is obnoxious in the play. He has no redeeming features, unlike, say, Musgrave's idealism or even the Mayor's lack of hypocrisy. Bludgeon is in favour of anything that offers him momentary gratification – and for that moment only:

> Old Joe looks out for Joe
> Plots and plans and who lies low?
> But the Lord provides, says Crooked Old Joe (p.41).

Thus he tells the colliers how to steal the Gatling gun, and having gained amusement and excitement from watching them attempting this, he gets another dose of amusement by betraying them to Musgrave and seeing them chased off. Here, as in the market-place scene, his changing sides according to self-interest is not exactly simple, but paradoxically it makes him seem the most inhumanly simple creature in the play – a creature of pure malice and self-interest, like a goblin or devil in a folk tale (an impression deepened by his physical crookedness as a hunchback, demonstrating his moral crookedness – an obvious symbolism Arden does not use for his complex characters). Paradoxically again, this creature does stand as a warning against the self-interested, irrationally evil sides of human nature, qualifying the good qualities we find in Annie and Mrs Hitchcock. He mimics the behaviour of Musgrave when praying and when coping with Sparky's death, he is mockingly deferential to the Parson, he teases and provokes the colliers and Annie, and he generally brings out everyone's bad points, making us look askance at their good points. Perhaps there is some justification for Musgrave's trying to control the anarchy of life after all, when it displays the vices thrown into relief by the Bargee.

Origins

The origins of *Serjeant Musgrave's Dance* are of two kinds – elements that immediately inspired the play; and a wider area of influences upon Arden which affected the various choices that he made in planning his material. One of the immediate influences was a violent incident in Cyprus, then occupied by British troops, in October 1958.

> A soldier's wife was shot in the street by terrorists – and according to newspaper reports – which was all I had to work on at the time – some soldiers ran wild at night and people were killed in the rounding-up. The atrocity which sparks off Musgrave's revolt, and which happens before the play begins, is roughly similar. (*Encore* No 32, 1961, p.31)

Another immediate influence was his reaction to the staging of his own previous play, *Live Like Pigs*, which, although dealing with the kind of unpredictable, unconventional modern characters who would be called 'colourful', was not, in his opinion, *visually* colourful:

> The first idea for the play [*Musgrave*] came to me in stage terms partly because of its spectacle. I had seen a number of contemporary plays and felt – particularly with *Live Like Pigs* – well, this is all very nice, I like this play, but I can see, looking at it on the stage why some people don't like it. It *is* grey. And I suddenly wanted to write a play with a visual excitement as well as a verbal one. I visualised the stage full of scarlet uniforms, and began to get interested from there. (*Encore* No. 32, 1961, p.40)

So he set his violent military incident in the nineteenth century, before the British army had changed from scarlet uniforms to present day khaki. Therefore Musgrave's character had to fit in with this period; Arden decided that 'the most likely character would be one of those Crimean Sergeants, who fought with rifle in one hand and a bible in the other', whereas 'if I had made Musgrave into a straightforward liberal, with whom our modern progressives would immediately feel at home, he would have been historically out of the picture, and most unlikely as a sergeant in the Victorian Army'. (*Encore* No. 32, 1961, p.31)

The way the plot unfolds as a classic 'strangers rode into town' situation, whereby new elements are introduced into a closed community, came to Arden from a film, *The Raid*, set during the American Civil War between Southern Confederate forces and Northern forces in the mid-nineteenth century:

> The plan of the film is rather similar: a group of them – Confederate soldiers in disguise – ride into a Northern town. Three-quarters of the film is taken up with their installation in the town, and the various personal relationships they establish. On the appointed morning they all turn out in their Confederate uniforms, hoist a flag in the square, rob the bank and burn the houses. Finally, as in *Serjeant Musgrave*, the cavalry arrives at the last minute although in this case they are too late. (*Encore* No. 32, 1961, p.26)

This is one particular influence that Arden was aware of, but in the same way he is of course drawing on his wide knowledge of literature, theatre of all kinds, film, painting and so on. For instance, he inserts several ballad-style verses and songs into the play, specifying what traditional folk-song airs the songs should be sung to, because 'The bedrock of English poetry is the ballad' which goes back at least to medieval times by way of the music hall song of Victorian England, and, he says, 'It seems to me that this tradition is the one that will always in the end reach to the heart of the people, even if the people are not entirely aware of what it is that causes their response' (*Encore* No. 25, 1960, p.24) – as opposed to the general view that the theatre is only for the privileged and 'cultured'. And apart from the 'ballads' that he includes, the characters and situation correspond to those in certain traditional ballads, as is discussed later.

Arden himself refers to other broad dramatic traditions, describing the play as being 'based on a combination of Elizabethan tragedy and nineteenth-century melodrama'. Serjeant Musgrave is an impressive and dominating personality and conforms to the classic definition of the tragic hero, in that he is in a position of power and is brought low because of a fatal flaw in his own character. As in Shakespeare's plays, including the tragedies, the action keeps moving from one location to another – the canal bank to the pub to the graveyard and back to the pub – as opposed to the convenient and economical single sets favoured increasingly as scenery became more realistic. Arden explains that he did not write wholly in verse because the twentieth-century theatre is not as formal an activity as it used to be, whereas 'the Elizabethans were able to write largely in verse because the theatre in those days was a much more formal activity than it is now'. He points out that nevertheless his characters do make use of the convention of speaking verse at moments of intense feeling, as when Annie breaks into a 'four-stanza spoken ballad' about her feelings towards soldiers: 'she is also speaking out of an emotional pressure, and therefore can drop into verse without any difficulty at all' (*Encore* No. 32, 1961, p.29). Even in the prose speeches, the stark imagery is strongly reminiscent of Shakespeare's equally bold and colourful images of blood, fire, blackness.

Victorian melodrama too used many of the elements of tragedy and of ballad in a popular way. Familiar themes were the plight of the abandoned sweetheart and the confrontation of tyrant and victim – a powerful plot element in all traditions, whether it is Macbeth plotting to eliminate disloyal lords, the melodrama's cruel landlord threatening a poor tenant's family, or the Mayor planning to use the soldiers to quell his miners.

To these influences one could add that of film techniques generally, apart from the plot of *The Raid*: films cut from one scene to another effortlessly, and the movement between the stable and Musgrave's bedroom within the stable scene would be particularly suited to film. A modern playwright whom Arden admires, Bertolt Brecht, also used the short, episodic scene, each making its own point; Brecht's theory that an audience should remain critically aware enough to assess the rightness and wrongness of his characters' behaviour throughout the action is shared by Arden (see quotation on page xiii).

But the similarities and echoes from past and contemporary works does not mean that *Serjeant Musgrave's Dance* therefore belongs to one particular 'school' of technique or thought. It is as well to notice also the *differences* which demarcate Arden's play from other plays and films. The characters in Musgrave are obviously more fully drawn, have greater dimension to their lives, than the bold but simple figures of ballad or melodrama (or toy theatre, or theatrical portrait, which Arden also admired for their boldness). And the informality of the very natural speech in which the colourful images are embedded links the play with realistic modern conventions, as opposed to Elizabethan formality.

On the other hand, this informality and naturalness is interrupted by enough melodramatic and ballad elements, as has been shown to distinguish it from the total, detailed, eavesdropping type of naturalism that is the normal style of films. And the simultaneity of drama – the fact that the audience can see the whole stage at once while different things are happening, as in the opening when Sparky's songs and comments provoke anxious reactions (visually as well as verbally) from the separate pair of card-playing soldiers – is a quality that Arden uses far more than he uses focus on individuals in isolation.

Melodrama too usually turns on a highly conventional, simple moral message, which *Serjeant Musgrave's Dance* emphatically does not; and the short scenes of Brecht's plays don't carry over mystery and suspense as does Arden's plot. So it would be wrong to deduce from these influences that *Serjeant Musgrave's Dance* is 'just like the Elizabethan drama' or 'borrowed from Brecht' or 'just like ballad': each element must be assessed for its particular effect, and for its interaction (by contrast or reinforcement) with the other elements.

Verbal and visual poetry

'Poetry in the theatre is a delicate lace, impossible to see at any distance. Poetry of the theatre should be a coarse lace, a lace of ropes, a ship at sea.'

Jean Cocteau

Stage imagery

Serjeant Musgrave's Dance has both 'poetry in the theatre' in Cocteau's sense in that its dialogue is often poetic; and 'poetry of the theatre' because actions and other visual elements remind us of or affect us like poetry. The latter are probably amongst the effects Arden had in mind when he said that he wanted to write a less grey, more visually exciting play. Like Cocteau he saw action as robustly poetic:

> What I am deeply concerned with is the problem of translating the concrete life of today into terms of poetry that shall at the one time both illustrate that life and set it within the historical and legendary tradition of our culture. (*Encore* No. 25, 1960, p.22)

In fact he first began writing the play with three visual images, as 'almost "given" scenes – from the "muse" if you like' (*Encore* No. 32, 1961, p.37), these being the soldiers' arrival, the stable scene, and he market place scene. The opening tableau of the mysterious soldiers grouped by twilight, on the watch against unknown danger, is a romantic and poetic one, as is their meeting in the churchyard where reports from east, west and south echo each other in action as well as in the ballad-like repetition of their words, each beginning 'Hardly a thing, street empty . . . ' (p.28). The stable scene also has ballad-like repetition in Annie's approach to the three soldiers in turn, enacted in their separate areas of the shadowy stable. Then in the market place all the main characters form another tableau, raised on a platform and gathered around the focal point of the cross/ lamp/ post with its flag and later the sudden and shocking hoisting of the skeleton. Again there is reference to ballads, as Annie takes down the skeleton and in a poignant and easily visualised stage picture, sits singing under the cross. An essential quality of ballads is the strong simple language and clear-cut images in which the stories are expressed. As Arden says

> In the ballads the colours are primary. Black is for death, and for the coalmines. Red is for murder, and for the soldier's coat the collier puts on to escape from his black. Blue is for the sky and for the sea that parts true love. Green fields are speckled with bright flowers. The seasons are clearly defined. White winter, green spring, golden summer, red autumn. (*Encore* No. 25, 1960, p.24)

This strong colouring focuses attention on the soldier's strange quest; as strangers in the town they are made conspicuous by their scarlet coats in the dingy grey streets. As the dialogue reminds us, they are 'on the run, in red uniforms, on a black-and-white coalfield' (p.29). Black, white and red are the colours of the playing cards being used as the play opens, and the game is a symbol for what will happen in the action: 'The black spades carry the day. Jack, King and Ace. *We* throw the red Queen over' (p.9). In popular fortune-telling by playing cards, the red Queen of Hearts stands for love, and we do indeed see how Black Jack Musgrave sweeps aside love. (Conversely, the Queen of Spades, later drawn by Annie in the pub scene, stands for trouble.)

But apart from colour, and the 'set-piece' tableaux, briefer moments of visual excitement keep arising from the course of the play, such as the Bargee's mimicking of Musgrave's prayer like a malevolent shadow, the jerky 'Fred Karno' mock drill by the colliers, the moment of Sparky's death emerging from the soldiers' confused scuffle. These do not mean that the play is a 'poetic drama' in the way that the verse plays of poets T.S. Eliot and Christopher Fry were a conscious attempt to revive a 'poetic drama' in the decade following World War II; instead they form moments of poetry *in* a drama.

> . . . the dialogue can be naturalistic and 'plotty' as long as the basic poetic issue has not been crystallised. But when this point is reached, then the language becomes formal (if you like, in verse, or sung), the visual pattern coalesces into a vital image that is one of the nerve-centres of the play. (*Encore* No. 25, 1960, p.25)

Poetic language

'This is a realistic, but not a naturalistic, play' (p.5) begins Arden's introduction to *Serjeant Musgrave's Dance.* He is making a distinction between two critical terms which are sometimes used as if they meant the same thing: the distinction (as most critics agree, though some confusingly make exactly the opposite definition) is between realism as a style which conforms generally to everyday life – the characters do not behave in an exaggerated or unexpected way, they do not move balletically or bound around the stage acrobatically as in pantomime, nor does the action include impossible or supernatural or dream-like elements – and naturalism, in which the environment and normal behaviour of the characters is displayed at length and in detail for its own sake, to make a point about the interaction of environment and character. In this play, the language is mainly a north-of-England dialect for the townspeople (except the Parson) and a similar dialect for the soldiers (though they are often played as having accents of different regions of the British Isles). It is therefore realistic in representing what men do say in situations like those that arise – as among the drunken colliers, or in Musgrave's casual, almost chatty opening to his 'recruiting speech'. And without departing from this convincing realism the language is vivid and original. The characters draw imagery from ordinary objects, as when Annie links the desolation of her bereavement with Billy's death and with the baby's deformity by saying 'A little withered clover – three in one it made' (p.63), or when she mocks at the soldiers' constant references to Musgrave: 'that serjeant squats in your gobs like an old wife stuck in a fireplace' (p.62). Arden admired both Ben Jonson and Dickens for their fantasy of language, 'piling ideas on ideas until a kind of *reductio ad absurdum* is reached' (*To Present the Pretence*, p.30) and there is something of this in the way he makes Musgrave criticise his men's slowness, not by saying just 'what a shower' (p.73) (what a generally inefficient group of men), but 'what a shower of tortoises' which not only specifies slowness but brings in a surreal vision of tortoises raining from the sky. Similarly, the Bargee's 'you'd be as well off wi' a row of deaf niggers from Peru' (p.12) trebles the idea of non-comprehension far more than if he had merely said 'deaf men'.

The prose gains its vigour not only from imagery but from rhythm. The townspeople tend to talk in short, fairly abrupt sentences, especially Mrs Hitchcock and the Mayor. They don't waste words on polite turns of phrase, and often leave the listener to make the connection between sentences, as in the Mayor's 'Red coats and flags. Get rid o' the trouble-makers. Drums and fifes and glory' (p.22). Musgrave also uses short sentences that show his efficiency and secrecy, as well as the fact that he is obviously not by nature a chatty sociable man, though he can use an easy, practised kind of army rhetoric, as in 'it's not what sends me here, and it's not what put *these* on my arm, and it's nowt at all to do with *my* life, or these two with me, or any o' yours' (p.81). However this rhetoric becomes less easy and more forceful when punctuated by the drumrolls as he reaches the climax of his speech. And when Musgrave's speech gets more urgent, taking a turn that the townspeople had not expected, he stops and marks the hoisting of the skeleton with his dance, and breaks into a song, usually performed as an emphatic chant.

But speech and chant are quite different, says Arden:

> . . . I prefer to make a firm distinction. I see prose as being a more useful vehicle for conveying plot and character relationships; and poetry as a sort of comment on them. (*Encore* No. 32, 1961)

Thus Annie comments on her feelings about soldiers in a ballad, and at the end Attercliffe comments on his own experiences (already described once in prose) in the final ballad. The point is, as Arden says, to make the verse quite clearly verse, which the characters are consciously reciting as verse, rather than have them speaking verse and pretending it was ordinary speech, which would obviously not be realistic.

> Some people might have thought that Musgrave's speech in the market place could be a suitable occasion to use verse. I did not, because at that point he has to present a certain amount of factual information concerning the massacre and so forth. Moreover, he is doing it in the role of a recruiting sergeant. Now a recruiting sergeant who speaks verse is a little awkward . . . If Musgrave had suddenly broken off and started talking verse too soon, it would have been wrong. (*Encore* No. 32, 1961, p.29)

Indeed, though the play *is* on the whole realistic, it is not entirely realistic – and certainly would not be naturalistic – to have so many of the characters ready to sing appropriate songs or to recite relevant pieces of verse. In ordinary life there tends to be more admixture of the everyday and the insignificant, whereas here, because of the play's basis in ballad, the 'costumes, movements, verbal patterns, music, must all be strong, and hard at the edges' (*Encore* No. 29, 1960, p.24). This is true of the verses spoken by the various characters, such as Mrs Hitchcock's

> I am a proud coal owner
> And in scarlet here I stand. (p.15)

or Sparky's

> She came to me at midnight
> With the moonshine on her arms . . . (p.58)

or Musgrave's chanted

> But white and red
> He waves his head . . . (p.85)

or Attercliffe's

> Your blood-red rose is withered and gone
> And fallen on the floor . . . (p.103).

All these are easily visualised images, and most of them contain the word 'red' or 'scarlet'. These bold contrasts reappear in the imagery of the ordinary prose dialogue at times, especially when the characters are excited:

> . . . stand before this people with our white shining word, and let it dance! It's a hot coal, this town, despite that it's freezing – choose your minute and blow: and whoosh, she's flamed your roof off! (pp.35-6)

It is not only metaphorically that Serjeant Musgrave 'sees things in black and white'; literally for him duty is 'drawn out straight and black for us, a clear plan' (p.51) as in both the army 'book' of rules, and the Bible. The strong outlines and hard edges of ballad were approved by Arden for any play based on ballad themes, however interpreted, but in the case of *Serjeant Musgrave's Dance,* where the main theme turns on Musgrave's harshness and inflexibility, this starkness of expression fits the nature of the conflict perfectly.

Critical reception

The most remarkable thing to emerge from surveying reactions to successive productions of *Serjeant Musgrave's Dance* is not that the critics find the play hard to understand, but that their second viewing or reading revealed the play as perfectly clear – and this is usually the experience of the average member of the audience too.

1959

Thus Harold Hobson of the Sunday Times began his review 'Another dreadful ordeal' and retained an impression of great boredom. Eric Keown in *Punch* asked 'Why was this piece put on?' and concluded 'There might have been some felicities of dialogue or wit to leaven this lump of absurdity, but I failed to detect them'. And in retrospect Alan Brien who was one of those who liked it, wondered whether he had been won over by Jocelyn Herbert's sets – which, 'with their nightmarish draughtmanship created an obsessed, claustrophobic other-world, half Akerman print, and half German silent film' – rather than the merits of the play itself. In fact, as Caryl Brahms summed up in *Plays and Players*, some critics 'boasted that they could understand it but disliked it. Others have admitted that they could not understand it but disliked it'. She herself was of the 'enlightened few' who liked it, but she interpreted its 'message' as being simply that 'war was wicked and must cease', so the criticism of Musgrave's war-like anti-war methods was evidently still not at all clear even to the open-minded.

1965

By the time it was revived by the Royal Court in 1965, *Serjeant Musgrave's Dance* had 'been done by three quarters of the university dramatic societies in the country', and, Arden continued

> A lot of critics are taking back what they said at first – Harold Hobson changed his mind after seeing the University production at Leeds. To my annoyance they do so by denigrating the London production which I thought was an excellent one. It is a difficult play, but I wish they would accept the fact that they simply missed the point when they first saw it. (*Encore* No. 32, 1961, p.33)

Harold Hobson actually attributed the success of the 1965 revival to the actor playing Musgrave, Iain Cuthbertson: 'Could he save *Serjeant Musgrave's Dance*? He could and he did. I put the matter crudely in order to emphasise the extent of Mr. Arden's debt to

Mr. Cuthbertson.' Mervyn Jones in *Tribune* was clearer about the advantages of already knowing the play: 'so many hints "placed" in this play gain value when one can reach mentally forward.' Ronald Bryden, another who wondered if in 1959 he 'had been seduced by Jocelyn Herbert's stark, brilliant settings', attributed his better understanding to 'a clearer and firmer production', but not everyone agreed with this. 'What a splendid play!' exclaimed Martin Esslin in *Plays and Players* 'And what an unimaginative, limp production!' Others agreed that the play succeeded in spite of its 'ponderous' and 'funereal' production. Unfortunately some critics still saw the play as working 'on a crude and childish level' as did Hilary Spurling in the *Spectator,* who noted only that 'the case against violence' was put repeatedly.

1981

Everything seemed even clearer in 1981 in the successful National Theatre production, marking Arden's fiftieth birthday in 1980. The National's small adaptable Cottesloe auditorium was arranged with an open stage at one end and minimal sets to make the scene changes quick and easy. There was a white curtain, and a white cyclorama. As Mark Amory described it in the *Spectator,* 'the dominating colours are black, white and the scarlet of soldiers' uniforms: the few objects are made of stone, wood or steel'. This time most reviewers took care to spell out the paradox of Serjeant Musgrave's use of force against force, and to Robert Cushman in the *Observer* 'the closing note of fatalistic optimism (characters doomed, cause not) is beautifully judged'. Further enthusiasm was voiced by Michael Billington: 'This is a spell-binding mind-challenging drama that touches greatness; and what is more it is written in that wonderful Arden lanague that seems to be hewn out of granite'. But there were still dissatisfied, though not baffled, opinions; Dick Vosburgh in *Punch* found it 'portentous', Mark Amory regretted that there was no 'slam-bang ending' and Douglas Orgill would have liked to feel a 'sense of identity with Musgrave'. But these admitted many virtues in the play – the all-bad review was now very rare.

Peter Brook's Paris production 1963

In his book *Arden: A Study of His Plays* (Eyre Methuen 1974) Albert Hunt describes Peter Brook's 1963 production of *Serjeant Musgrave's Dance* in Paris in French, and noted how 'it proved impossible to translate into French the rich, colloquial, essentially northern flavour of Arden's language' (p.164), although Arden himself supervised the translation. Visually the red-black-white scheme was blurred because Brook's production 'was built around a grey-green motif' (p.166); a grey-green slab was used throughout the play for tombstones, stable divisions and so on, and at the end the dancing miners reappeared *after* the prison scene and after Attercliffe's last line about starting an orchard, thus leaving the audience with the image of the trapped unchanging miners, instead of hope. For Hunt, 'Brook had turned Arden's popular ballad into a statement of mid-century despair – the image of a nightmare that nobody can control. In doing so, he had created a brilliant theatrical experience – but had lost the point of the play' (p.167).

The colliers' clog dance (p.40) from the 1965 revival (*Photo: Dominic*)

Further reading

Arden's work

Most of John Arden's plays, as well as those written jointly with Margaretta D'Arcy (indicated below with an asterisk *), have been published by Methuen. The following titles are still in print in paperback (in the Methuen Modern Plays series):

Serjeant Musgrave's Dance, 1960
*The Business of Good Government**, 1963
The Workhouse Donkey, 1964
Armstrong's Last Goodnight, 1965
*The Royal Pardon**, 1967
*The Island of the Mighty**, 1974
Pearl, 1979
*Vandaleur's Folly**, 1981

Methuen also publish a paperback anthology in their Master Playwrights series:

Arden – Plays: One, 1977,

which contains *Serjeant Musgrave's Dance, The Workhouse Donkey* and *Armstrong's Last Goodnight*. A further paperback anthology is published by Penguin:

Three Plays, 1969,

which contains *The Waters of Babylon, Live Like Pigs* and *The Happy Haven*. Pluto Press have published (in three volumes):

The Non-Stop Connolly Show, 1978

Two further books are available in paperback;

Ironhand (Arden's adaptation of a play by Goethe, *Goetz von Berlichingen*), 1965
To Present the Pretence (Arden's own selection of his writings on the theatre), 1977

Both these are published by Methuen.

Background books

Anger and Detachment by Michael Anderson (1976) – a third of the book is devoted to Arden

Theatre Language by John Russell Brown (1972) – includes a chapter on Arden

John Arden by Ronald Hayman (1968) – 'Contemporary Dramatists' series
Arden: A Study of His Plays by Albert Hunt (1974)
Drama in the Sixties by Laurence Kitchin (1966) – includes a chapter on Arden
John Arden by Glenda Leeming (1974) – 'Writers and their Work' series
Anger and After by John Russell Taylor (revised edition 1969) – contains a chapter on Arden
John Arden by Simon Trussler (New York, 1973) – 'Columbia Essays on Modern Writers'

The Mayor and the soldiers (Musgrave far right) from the 1965 revival (*Photo: Dominic*)

INTRODUCTION

This is a realistic, but not a naturalistic, play. Therefore the design of the scenes and costumes must be in some sense stylised. The paintings of L. S. Lowry might suggest a suitable mood. Scenery must be sparing – only those pieces of architecture, furniture, and properties actually *used* in the action need be present: and they should be thoroughly realistic, so that the audience sees a selection from the details of everyday life rather than a generalised impression of the whole of it. A similar rule should also govern the direction and the acting. If this is done, the obvious difficulties, caused by the mixture of verse, prose, and song in the play, will be considerably lessened.

The exact date of the play is deliberately not given. In the London production, the details of costume covered approximately the years between 1860 and 1880. For instance, the soldiers wore the scarlet tunics and spiked helmets characteristic of the later (or 'Kipling') epoch, while the Constable was dressed in tall hat and tail coat as an early Peeler – his role in the play suggesting a rather primitive type of police organisation.

The songs should be sung to folk-song airs. There are many available tunes which equally well suit the various songs – perhaps these are as good as any:

Sparky's song (Act One, Scene 1): 'Six Jolly Wee Miners' – Scottish.

Sparky's song and chorus (Act Two, Scene 2): 'Blow away the Morning Dew' – English.

Sparky's song (Act Two, Scene 3): 'The Black Horse' – Irish.

Attercliffe's song (Act Three, Scene 2): First three stanzas – 'John Barleycorn' – English Air. Final stanza – 'John Barleycorn' – Irish Air.

Musgrave's song (Act Three, Scene 1) proved in production to be more satisfactory if the words were spoken against a background of drum rolls and recorded music.

The characters perhaps need a few notes of description:

The Soldiers: these are regulars and seasoned men. They should all have moustaches and an ingrained sense of discipline. Musgrave is aged between thirty and forty, tall, swart, commanding, sardonic but never humorous; he could well have served under Cromwell. Attercliffe is aged about fifty, grey-haired, melancholy, a little embittered. He is the senior O.R. of the party and conscious of his responsibility. Hurst, in his twenties, is bloody-minded, quick-tempered, handsome, cynical, tough, but not quite as intelligent as he thinks he is. Sparky, also in his twenties, is easily led, easily driven, inclined to hide from himself behind a screen of silly stories and irritating clownishness. The Dragoon Officer is little more than the deus-ex-machina at the end of the play. All he needs to be is tall, calm, cold, and commanding. His Trooper is a tough, reliable soldier.

The Townsmen: The Mayor is a bustling, shrewd, superficially jovial man with a coarse accent and an underlying inclination to bully. The Parson is very much a gentleman: he is conscious of the ungentlemanly nature of the community in which he lives. He must have the accent and manners of a balked aristocrat rather than a stage-clergyman. He too has some inclination to bully. The Constable has a continual inclination to bully, except when in the presence of his superiors. He is as inefficient as he is noisy. The Colliers are all embittered but not so as to make them unpleasant. Walsh is a strong man, physically and morally. He knows what he wants and is entirely impatient with those who are not so single-minded. The Slow Collier is not particularly intelligent but has a vacuous good humour. The Pugnacious Collier is pugnacious, and very quick to show it. The Bargee is something of a grotesque, a hunchback (though this should not be over-emphasised), very rapid in his movements, with a natural urge towards intrigue and mischief.

The Women: The Landlady is a large, immobile widow of about fifty. She sits behind her bar and watches everything that happens. She is clearly a woman of deep sympathies and intelligence, which she disguises with the normal north-country sombre pessimism. Annie is a big-boned girl, not particularly attractive, but in an aggressive sort of way she provokes the men. Her emotional confusion expresses itself in a deliberately enigmatic style of speech and behaviour. Her voice is harsh.

As for the 'Meaning of the Play': I do not think that an introductory note is a suitable place for a lengthy analysis of the work, but in view of the obvious puzzlement with which it was greeted by the critics, perhaps a few points may be made. This is not a nihilistic play. This is not (except perhaps unconsciously) a symbolist play. Nor does it advocate bloody revolution. I have endeavoured to write about the violence that is so evident in the world, and to do so through a story that is partly one of wish-fulfilment. I think that many of us must at some time have felt an overpowering urge to match some particularly outrageous piece of violence with an even greater and more outrageous retaliation. Musgrave tries to do this: and the fact that the sympathies of the play are clearly with him in his original horror, and then turn against him and his intended remedy, seems to have bewildered many people. I would suggest, however, that a study of the roles of the women, and of Private Attercliffe, should be sufficient to remove any doubts as to where the 'moral' of the play lies. Accusations of nihilism seem to derive from the scene where the Colliers turn away from Musgrave and join in the general dance around the beer barrel. Again, I would suggest, that an unwillingness to dwell upon unpleasant situations that do not immediately concern us is a general human trait, and recognition of it need imply neither cynicism nor despair. Complete pacifism is a very hard doctrine: and if this play appears to advocate it with perhaps some timidity, it is probably because I am naturally a timid man – and also because I know that if I am hit I very easily hit back: and I do not care to preach too confidently what I am not sure I can practise.

J.A.

Serjeant Musgrave's Dance was first performed at the Royal Court Theatre on 22 October 1959, with the following cast:

PRIVATE SPARKY	Donal Donnelly
PRIVATE HURST	Alan Dobie
PRIVATE ATTERCLIFFE	Frank Finlay
BLUDGEON, *a bargee*	James Bree
SERJEANT MUSGRAVE	Ian Bannen
THE PARSON	Richard Caldicot
MRS. HITCHCOCK	Freda Jackson
ANNIE	Patsy Byrne
THE CONSTABLE	Michael Hunt
THE MAYOR	Stratford Johns
A SLOW COLLIER	Jack Smethurst
A PUGNACIOUS COLLIER	Colin Blakely
WALSH, *an earnest collier*	Harry Gwynn Davies
A TROOPER OF DRAGOONS	Barry Wilsher
AN OFFICER OF DRAGOONS	Clinton Greyn

Produced by LINDSAY ANDERSON
Music by DUDLEY MOORE
Decor by JOCELYN HERBERT

The play is set in a mining town in the north of England eighty years ago. It is winter.

Act One

SCENE ONE

A canal wharf. Evening.

HURST *and* ATTERCLIFFE *are playing cards on the top of a side-drum. A few yards away* SPARKY *stands, as though on guard, clapping himself to keep warm. There is a pile of three or four heavy wooden boxes with the WD broad arrow stencilled on them, and a lantern set on top.*

SPARKY. Brr, oh a cold winter, snow, dark. We wait too long, that's the trouble. Once you've started, keep on travelling. No good sitting to wait in the middle of it. Only makes the cold night colder. (*He sings*):

One day I was drunk, boys, on the Queen's Highway
When a recruiting party come beating that way.
I was enlisted and attested before I did know
And to the Royal Barracks they forced me to go.

Brr! And they talk of the Crimea! Did I ever tell you that one about the field kitchens at Sebastopol? Well, there was this red-haired provost-sarnt, y'see . . . and then the corporal-cook – now *he'd* got no hair at all . . . now the Commissary in that Regiment was – oh . . . (*He finds no one paying attention.*) Who's winning?

HURST. I'm winning.

ATTERCLIFFE. Oho, no you're not. The black spades carry the day. Jack, King and Ace. *We* throw the red Queen over. That's another shilling, you know. Let's have it.

HURST. All right. Deal agen, boy. Or no, no, *my* deal, this game. Now let's see if I can't turn some good cards on to my side for a difference. Here: one, two, three, four . . . (*He deals the cards.*)

SPARKY. How much longer we got to wait, I'd like to know. I want to be off aboard that damned barge and away. What's happened to our Black Jack Musgrave, eh? Why don't he come and give us the word to get going?

ATTERCLIFFE. He'll come on the stroke, as he said. He works his life to bugle and drum, this serjeant. You ever seen him late?

SPARKY. No. (*He sings*):

> When first I deserted I thought myself free
> Till my cruel sweetheart informed upon me –

ATTERCLIFFE (*sharply*). I don't think you ought to sing *that* one.

SPARKY. Why not? It's true, isn't it? (*He sings*):

> Court martial, court martial, they held upon me
> And the sentence they passed was the high gallows tree.

HURST (*dropping cards and springing up in a rage*). Now shut it, will you! God-damned devil of a song to sing on this sort of a journey! He said you didn't ought to, so don't! (*He glances nervously around.*)

SPARKY. Ha, there's nobody to hear us. You're safe as a bloody blockhouse out here – I'm on the sentry, boy, *I'm* your protection.

ATTERCLIFFE (*irritably*). You make sure you are then. Go on: keep watching.

SPARKY (*returns to his guard*). Ah. Ha-ha . . . Or did you think *he* could hear you? (*He gestures towards the boxes.*) Maybe, maybe . . . *I* thought I heard him laugh.

ATTERCLIFFE. Steady, boy.

SPARKY (*a little wildly*). Steady yourself, you crumbling old cuckold. He might laugh, who knows? Well, make a rattling any road. Mightn't he, soldier boy?

HURST. Are you coming funny wi' me –

SPARKY. Funny? About *him*? You don't tell me he don't know what we're at. Why shouldn't he have a laugh at it, if that's how he feels?

HURST. Arrh, you're talking daft.

SPARKY. Now don't you be nervous, boy: not for *you* to be nervous. You're a man and a soldier! Or an old red rag stretched over four pair o' bones – well, what's the odds? Eh?

HURST (*after glaring angrily, sits down again*). *All right* . . . All right, play.

They play in silence. SPARKY *hums and blows his knuckles. Then he starts.*

SPARKY. Who goes there!

The BARGEE *enters with a lantern, whistling 'Michael Finnegan'.*

BARGEE. Hooroar, my jolly buckos! It's only old Joe Bludgeon, the Captain of the Lugger. Crooked old Joe. Heh heh. And what's the news with you? Are we ready yet, are we?

SPARKY. Ready for what?

BARGEE. Ready for off, of course, what do you think? Are we?

ATTERCLIFFE. No.

BARGEE. Why not, then?

ATTERCLIFFE. 'Cos it's not time, that's why not. Half-past seven, you was told.

BARGEE. Oh, it's as near as –

ATTERCLIFFE. No begod it's not, and he won't be here till it is.

BARGEE. Ah, the serjeant, eh?

ATTERCLIFFE. Aye, the serjeant. Is your barge up yet?

BARGEE. It's up. And the old horse waiting.

ATTERCLIFFE. Then we'll start to load.

HURST. Hey, we've not finished the game.

ATTERCLIFFE. Save it, mucker. You heard what Black Jack said.

HURST. All right. All right.

BARGEE. You can load these smaller cases 'side of the cabin. What you got in 'em, for Godsake? Ten ton and a half here.

SPARKY (*kicking one of them*). There's a Gatling gun in that one. You know what a Gatling gun is, friend?

BARGEE. I don't, and I don't care neither, tell you truth of it. By Lordy, what a life, the bloody Army. Do they still tie you fellers up and stripe you across with the cat-o'-nine-tails, eh?

HURST. No they don't.

ATTERCLIFFE *and* HURST *start carrying the cases out.*

BARGEE (*gloating*). Heheh, when I wor a young lad they told me, they did. Whack, whack, whack. Ooh, cruel it was. You know what they used to call 'em in them days – soldiers, I mean? Eh?

SPARKY. I know a lot o' names for calling soldiers.

BARGEE. I'll bet you don't know this one, though. Heh. Bloodred roses, that was it. What d'you think o' that, eh? Whack, whack, whack. Bloodred roses, eh? (*He calls off-stage.*) Not there, don't put it there, give me some room to swing me tiller, can't you! Soldiers. Get 'em aboard a barge, you'd be as well off wi' a row of deaf niggers from Peru. That's right, now leave it where you've dropped it, and come ashore before you capsize her—you bloodred bloody roses, you!

HURST *re-enters.*

HURST. That's enough of that, matey. Watch it.

MUSGRAVE *enters.*

MUSGRAVE (*to the* BARGEE). Aye, you watch it. Now I'll tell you just once, old man, and that's all. We travel on your barge, passengers: we pay our fare. So don't you talk to my men like they're deck-hands. Clear?

BARGEE. Oh it's clear, serjeant, I only wanted a little joke.

MUSGRAVE. Aye. And now you've had one. So be thankful.

ATTERCLIFFE *re-enters.*

ATTERCLIFFE (*as he and* HURST *pick up the remaining smaller boxes*). We got the Gatling loaded on serjeant, and we're fetching the rest of it. Then there's just the drum and the other box left. Any news?

MUSGRAVE (*quietly to him*). We're all all right. Don't worry.

ATTERCLIFFE *and* HURST *go out with their load.* MUSGRAVE *taps the drum meditatively and turns to the* BARGEE.

I say, you, bargee. Is it going to snow again before to-morrow?

BARGEE. Likely. There's ice coming on the water too. Give her another day and this canal'll be closed. They say the road over the moors is fast already with the drifts. You've chose a merry time o' year beating up for recruities, haven't you? What you got in here? Another Gatling gun? (*He smacks the last box.*)

MUSGRAVE. Why not? Show 'em all the best equipment, glamourise 'em, man, fetch 'em in like conies . . . Now get this last box loaded, and be careful. And then we're all ready. You can start.

ATTERCLIFFE *and* HURST, *having returned, pick up the box and carry it out,* SPARKY *going with them, the drum slung on his shoulder.* MUSGRAVE *takes the soldiers' lantern and makes a rapid circuit of the stage to see if anything is left. He stands for a moment looking out in the direction from which he has come in.*

BARGEE (*waiting for him*). This your first trip to the coal-mining towns, serjeant?

MUSGRAVE. It is.

BARGEE. Ooh, brr, bitter and bleak: hungry men for the Queen. If you're used to a full belly, you'll want it when you get there.

MUSGRAVE (*curtly*). It's not material. We have our duty. A soldier's duty is a soldier's life.

BARGEE. Ah, duty.

The Empire wars are far away
For duty's sake we sail away
Me arms and legs is shot away
And all for the wink of a shilling and a drink . . .

Come on, me cheery serjeant, you've not left nowt behind.

They go out after the soldiers.

SCENE TWO

The bar of a public house.

MRS. HITCHCOCK *is sitting in the body of the room, talking to the* PARSON, *who is very much at his ease, with a glass of brandy in his hand.* ANNIE *is polishing glasses etc. behind the bar.*

PARSON. No. No, madam, no. I cannot be seen to countenance idleness, pauperism, beggary. If no one comes to buy your drink, I am sorry for you. But the fact is, madam, a little less drunkenness and disorder will do this town no harm. The Church is not a speculative bank, you know, to subsidise pot-houses.

MRS. HITCHCOCK (*sulkily*). Always a respectable house.

PARSON. What?

MRS. HITCHCOCK. Always a respectable house, reverend. Aye. If not, why renew the licence? You're a magistrate, you know. You could have spoke agen me on me application. But you didn't.

PARSON. That is not to the purpose, Mrs. Hitchcock. The Bench allows that there have to be public houses to permit an outlet for the poorer sort of people, but in times of regrettable industrial conflict it is better that as many of them as possible remain empty. If the colliers cannot afford drink because of the strike – because of their own stupidity – then there is the less likelihood of their being inflamed to acts of violence. I am not at all certain that the Bench ought not to withdraw all licences altogether until the pits are working.

MRS. HITCHCOCK. That'd be grand. See half a dozen publicans going on the parish – beer-dregs from the workhouse served to the Trade – ooh, talk of arsy-versy! (*She laughs throatily.*)

PARSON. I'm quite sure that would not be necessary.

MRS. HITCHCOCK (*reasonably*). Now, look, reverend, you've been taking me crossroads since the minute I began. All I asked you in to say is this: this strike is bad for the town. Well, I mean, of course, that means me. But it means you too. *And* it means His Worship the Mayor: oh aye, aye:

I am a proud coalowner
And in scarlet here I stand.
Who shall come or who shall go
Through all my coal-black land?

(*She laughs again.*) Eh, if we can't have a laugh, we'll starve!

PARSON. You are impertinent. I have nothing more to say.

MRS. HITCHCOCK. Ah, but I come to you because you're Church, you're charity. Go on, reverend, you tell the Mayor to agree with his men and give them a good price, then they'll buy and sell in the town and they'll drink in this taproom, and – ho-hoo – who knows, they might even come to church! That'll be the day.

The PARSON *turns irritably from her and goes to the door. The* BARGEE *enters and confronts him.*

BARGEE (*touching his cap mockingly*). Parson.

PARSON (*coldly*). Good afternoon.

BARGEE. Cold enough for you, eh?

PARSON (*trying to pass*). It is cold, yes.

BARGEE. How's the strike?

PARSON. It is not yet settled.

BARGEE. No, I bet it's not, and all. Hey missus!

MRS. HITCHCOCK. Hello.

BARGEE. A quart o' taddy. Best!

MRS. HITCHCOCK (*impassive*). Can you pay for it?

BARGEE. 'Course I can pay – wait a minute, Parson, just a minute, all under control – I'm not one of your colliery agitators, you know. *I'm* still in work. I've news for you.

MRS. HITCHCOCK (*to* ANNIE). He says he can pay. Draw him his quart.

BARGEE (*to the* PARSON). I didn't think, like, to find you here, but, eh, well, seeing as how here you are – canal's froze up, you know.

PARSON. Well?

BARGEE. Well. Last barge come in this morning. *My* barge. There was passengers.

PARSON. I am not really interested.

BARGEE (*significantly*). Four on 'em, Parson. Soldiers.

ANNIE *hands the* BARGEE *his tankard.*

PARSON (*in some alarm*). Soldiers! Already? Who sent for them? Why was I not told? This could be very dangerous –

BARGEE. They're not here for what you think, you know. Not yet, any road. You see, they've come recruiting.

PARSON (*relieved, but vexed*). Oh . . . Well, what if they have? Why bother me with it? You're just wasting time, man. Come on, get out of my way . . .

BARGEE (*still detaining him*). Eh, but, Parson, you're a magistrate.

PARSON. Of course I'm a magistrate.

BARGEE. You're a power, you are: in a town of trouble, in a place of danger. Yes. You're the word and the book, aren't you? Well then: soldiers. Recruiting. Useful?

PARSON (*beginning to follow his drift*). H'm. I do not think the Bench is in any real need of *your* suggestions. But I am obliged to you for the news. Thank you.

He gives the BARGEE *a coin and leaves.*

BARGEE (*flipping the coin*). Heh, heh, I said I could pay.

He gives it to ANNIE *and starts whistling 'Michael Finnegan'.* ANNIE *goes back to the bar.* MRS. HITCHCOCK *takes the coin from her and tests it between her teeth.*

MRS. HITCHCOCK. Soldiers. Annie, love, you could tell us what soldiers is good for.

ANNIE (*sullen*). Why should I tell you?

BARGEE (*gleefully*). Go on, go on, lassie, tell us about the soldiers. She knows the good redcoat button-to-back, I'll bet. Go on, it's a cold day, warm it up for us. Heh, heh, our strong Annie's the champion, eh?

He smacks her on the bottom. She swerves angrily.

ANNIE. *When* I've given you leave: and not afore. You bloody dog, sit down.

BARGEE (*subsiding in mock terror*). Ooh, sharp, sharp.

MRS. HITCHCOCK. Aye, so sit down . . . Go on, Annie, tell us.

ANNIE. I'll tell you for what a soldier's good:

> To march behind his roaring drum,
> Shout to us all: 'Here I come
> I've killed as many as I could –
> I'm stamping into your fat town

From the war and to the war
And every girl can be my whore
Just watch me lay them squealing down.
And that's what he does and so do we.
Because we know he'll soon be dead
We strap our arms round the scarlet red
Then send him weeping over the sea.
Oh he will go and a long long way.
Before he goes we'll make him pay
Between the night and the next cold day –
By God there's a whole lot more I could say –

What good's a bloody soldier 'cept to be dropped into a slit in the ground like a letter in a box. How many did you bring with you – is it four?

BARGEE. Aye. Four.

ANNIE. That's four beds in this house?

MRS. HITCHCOCK. I should hope it's in this house. It's the best house in town.

ANNIE (*in a sudden outburst*). Then you'd do well to see they stay four nights because I'll not go with more nor one in one night, no, not for you nor for all of Egypt!

She lets out a howl and rushes out of the door behind the bar, clattering a tin tray full of tankards on to the floor.

BARGEE. Ooh, Lordy! Champion, strong, and sharp. Annie! Tell us some more!

MRS. HITCHCOCK (*crossly*). Let her alone. She's said enough for you, hasn't she? It's not right to set her off . . . I suppose they *are* coming to this house?

BARGEE. Oh surely, aye, surely. *I* told 'em: *I* took care.

A rat-tat-tat on the drum heard, off.

There, you see, they're coming.

SPARKY *enters magnificently, beating the drum.*

SPARKY. Ho-ho, atten-tion! Stand by your beds! Name of the Queen, missus – has he told you – there's four on us: we three, we'll settle for palliasses in the loft, but the serjeant he wants a big brass bed with knobs on, that's his fancy! Can you do it?

MRS. HITCHCOCK. So here they are, the gay recruiters. Aye, I can do it, young man. I've only one room in the house. The serjeant can have that. The three of you'll have to doss down in me old stable, out back, but there's a good stove, you'll be warm. Now, who's going to pay? You or the Queen?

SPARKY. Oh, Queen at end of it all, I suppose.

MRS. HITCHCOCK. But you at beginning, eh?

SPARKY. Oh-oh, chalk it up, you know . . . we've brought some gear with us too.

BARGEE. Ten and a half ton. Nigh foundered the old barge, it did, I can tell you.

SPARKY. But we got here, friend, didn't we? Like we get ourselves to everywhere we go, we do. No question o' that, y'see.

BARGEE. Heh, heh, none.

SPARKY (*calls to offstage*). Serjeant! We're fixed!

MUSGRAVE (*off*). And the equipment?

SPARKY. And the equipment, missus?

MRS. HITCHCOCK. There's a coach-house across the yard.

SPARKY (*calls to offstage*). Coach-house across the yard, serjeant! . . . While they're taking it round there, missus, let's have a pint apiece drawn ready. Like what *he* drinks, eh? Recommend it, friend?

BARGEE. You could stand your bayonet up in this, you could.

SPARKY. Right, then. And we'll give you another while we're at it. That's five on 'em, pints, unless *you're* drinking with us, too, are you?

MRS. HITCHCOCK. Why not, soldier? Queen as pays . . . Annie! Hey Annie!

As there is no reply, she goes herself behind the bar and starts filling the tankards. MUSGRAVE *enters.*

MUSGRAVE. Is the padlock on your coach-house door a strong one, ma'am?

MRS. HITCHCOCK. Likely so.

MUSGRAVE. Valuable equipment, y'see. Your window in there's barred, I notice.

MRS. HITCHCOCK. That's right.

MUSGRAVE (*picking up a tankard*). Good . . . This for me?

MRS. HITCHCOCK. If you want it.

The other two soldiers enter.

ATTERCLIFFE. The cases are all locked up and safe, serjeant.

MUSGRAVE (*indicates drinks*). Very good. Here you are.

HURST and ATTERCLIFFE. Thank you, serjeant.

BARGEE (*raising his drink*). Good health to Her Majesty; to Her Majesty's wars; to the girls we leave behind us. Drink!

They all drink.

MRS. HITCHCOCK (*raising her drink*):

Into the river, out of the river
Once I was dry, now I am wet
But hunger and cold they hold me yet.

They drink again, with a certain puzzlement at the toast.

MRS. HITCHCOCK. They hold this town today, any road, serjeant; or had you been told?

MUSGRAVE. What's the matter?

MRS. HITCHCOCK. No work in the colliery. The owner calls it a strike, the men call it a lock-out, we call it starvation.

The CONSTABLE *enters violently.*

CONSTABLE. His Worship the Mayor.

MRS. HITCHCOCK. Eh?

CONSTABLE. I said, His Worship the Mayor!

BARGEE. Oho, *now*, me jolly buckos, give attention, stand-to, to the present!

CONSTABLE (*to the* BARGEE]. Ssssh – ssh –

BARGEE. Heh, heh, heh –

The MAYOR *enters at speed, wearing his gold chain. After him comes the* PARSON. MUSGRAVE *calls his men to attention.*

MAYOR. Mrs. Hitchcock, I'm seeking the soldiers. Ah, here they are! Well, I'm the Mayor of this town, I own the colliery, I'm a worried man. So I come seeking you when I could send for you, what do you think to that? Let's have a look at you . . . Ah. Haha . . . Clear the snug a minute, missus. I want a private word with the Parson. Serjeant, be ready outside when I send for you.

MUSGRAVE. At your service, sir . . . Come on.

Beckoned by MRS. HITCHCOCK, *he leads his party out behind the bar.*

CONSTABLE (*propelling the* BARGEE *to the street door*). Go on, you, out this road.

BARGEE (*dodging him*). Oo-er –

Constable Constable alive or dead
His head is of leather and his belly's of lead.

Go – whoops . . . How are you, Parson?

He ducks out, whistling 'Michael Finnegan'.

MRS. HITCHCOCK (*sourly, to the* MAYOR). Do you want a drink?

MAYOR. No.

MRS. HITCHCOCK. *At* your service, when you do.

She curtsies and goes out behind the bar.

MAYOR. What do you think to 'em, Parson?

PARSON. Fine strong men. They make me proud of my country. Mr. Mayor, Britain depends upon these spirits. It is a great pity that their courage is betrayed at home by skulkers and shirkers. What do *you* think?

MAYOR (*looking at him sideways*). *I* think we'll use 'em, Parson. Temporary expedient, but it'll do. The price of coal has fell, I've had to cut me wages, I've had to turn men off. They say they'll strike, so I close me gates. We can't live like that for ever. There's two ways to solve this colliery – one is build the railway here and cut me costs of haulage, *that* takes two years and an Act of Parliament, though God knows I want to do it. The other is clear out half the population, stir up a diversion, turn their minds to summat else. The Queen's got wars, she's got rebellions. Over the sea. All right. Beat these fellers' drums high around the town, I'll put one pound down for every Royal Shilling the serjeant pays. Red coats and flags. Get rid o' the trouble-makers. Drums and fifes and glory.

PARSON (*severely*). The soldier's calling is one of honour.

MAYOR. It's more than that. It's bloody convenient. Town Constable, fetch that serjeant in!

CONSTABLE (*nervously*). Er, excuse me, Your Worship. A point. Soldiers, you see. Now, I've got a very small force in this town. Only one other regular officer, you know: the rest is them deputy-specials – I can't trust *that* lot to stand fast and fear nowt when the time comes.

PARSON. What time?

CONSTABLE. There's been stone-throwing this morning. Two of my office windows is broke. And I'm nervous—that's frank, you know – I *am*.

MAYOR. Well?

CONSTABLE. Your Worship. I want these soldiers added to my force. It's all right recruiting. But what we need's patrols.

MAYOR. Not yet.

CONSTABLE. Your Worship. I'm asking you formal. You've got agitators here, and they won't stop at throwing stones: that's frank.

MAYOR (*angrily*). I said not yet. We'll try it my road first. Godsake, man, what's four soldiers agen the lot of 'em? This town's wintered up, you'll get no more help till there's a thaw. So work on that. Call in the serjeant.

CONSTABLE. Right, Your Worship. Serjeant! Come in here!

MUSGRAVE *re-enters.*

MUSGRAVE. Sir?

MAYOR. Serjeant, we're very glad to have you. I speak for the Council, I speak for the magistrates. Now listen: there's loyal hearts and true here, and we're every man-jack of us keen to see our best lads flock to the colours. Isn't that so, Parson?

PARSON (*taken a little by surprise*). Ha-h'm – with great pride, yes.

MAYOR. Right. For every Queen's Shilling you give out, I give out a golden sovereign – no, two. One for the recruit, and one to be divided among you and your three good lads. What do you say to that?

MUSGRAVE. That's most handsome, sir.

MAYOR. I should damn well think it is. How do you propose to work?

MUSGRAVE. Sir?

MAYOR. Aye, I mean, d'you tramp around the streets drumming, or set on your fannies in a pub—or what?

MUSGRAVE. Depends what's most appropriate, sir, according to the type of town. I've not had time for a look at yours yet. But the pubs seem pretty empty, if this one's owt to go by.

PARSON. They *are* empty.

MUSGRAVE. Aye. Well, in that case, I'll have to make a reconnaissance, won't I? When I'm decided, I'll let you know.

CONSTABLE. And let me know, serjeant. I'll see you get facilities.

MUSGRAVE. Thank you, mister.

MAYOR. And while you're on about them facilities, constable, perhaps you might let in the serjeant on a few likely names for his list, eh? Could you pick him some passable strongset men, could you?

CONSTABLE (*significantly*). I could have a try, Your Worship.

MAYOR. Right. Then if that's settled, I'll be off back to town hall. I've not got time to waste wi' nattering, snug and all though it is in here. Come along, Constable. I want a little word wi' you about them stones.

MAYOR *and* CONSTABLE *go out.*

PARSON (*severely*). I think I ought to make one thing clear, serjeant. I know that it is customary for recruiting-parties to impress themselves upon the young men of the district as dashingly as possible, and no doubt upon the young women also. Now I am not having any of that. There's enough trouble in the place as it is. So remember.

MUSGRAVE. Yes, sir. I'll remember.

PARSON. I want no drunkenness, and no fornication, from your soldiers. Need I speak plainer?

MUSGRAVE. No, sir. There will be none. I am a religious man.

PARSON. Very well. Good day to you.

MUSGRAVE. Good day, sir.

The PARSON *goes.* MUSGRAVE *sits down, takes out a small pocket bible and reads.* MRS. HITCHCOCK *enters.*

MRS. HITCHCOCK. What, they've not all gone, already?

MUSGRAVE. They have, ma'am.

MRS. HITCHCOCK. Just like, isn't it? Use my bar for a council-parlour, leave nowt behind 'em but bad breath and a shiny bench – *they* take care. I'm giving your three their dinners in back. You eating with 'em?

MUSGRAVE (*of-handed*). No. I'll have a hand of bread and cheese and eat it here.

MRS. HITCHCOCK. Drink with it?

MUSGRAVE (*still at his book*). No . . . Thanks, no. Just the cheese.

MRS. HITCHCOCK (*sourly*). H'm, another on 'em . . . Hey, Annie! Slice o' bread and a piece o' cheese in here for this one! Pickles?

MUSGRAVE. Eh?

MRS. HITCHCOCK (*annoyed*). Pickles!

MUSGRAVE. No . . . (*He looks up suddenly.*) Tell me, ma'am, is there many from this town lately have gone for a soldier?

MRS. HITCHCOCK. Some. It's not a common pleasure here – not as long as the coal wor right to sell, any road. But there was some. You'll know the sort o' reasons, I daresay?

> The yellow-haired boy lay in my bed
> A-kissing me up from me toes to me head.
> But when my apron it did grow too short
> He thought it good time to leave his sport.

Enter ANNIE *with the bread and cheese. She gives it to* MUSGRAVE.

MUSGRAVE. Thank you.

ANNIE (*confronting him*). Serjeant you are.

MUSGRAVE. That's right.

ANNIE. You seem a piece stronger than the rest of 'em.

He nods.

And they call you Black Jack Musgrave?

He looks at her.

Well, I'm looking at your face, mister serjeant. Now do you know what I'd say?

MUSGRAVE. What?

ANNIE. The North Wind in a pair of millstones
Was your father and your mother
They got you in a cold grinding.
God help us all if they get you a brother.

She looks at him another minute, then nods her head and goes out.

MUSGRAVE (*wryly*). She talks a kind of truth, that lassie. Is she daft?

MRS. HITCHCOCK. No, no, no, I wouldn't say daft. But there's not many would let her bide in their house.

MUSGRAVE. Tell me, ma'am. It sticks on my mind that I once had a sort of a comrade came from this town. . . Long, yellow-haired lad, like in your little verse. Name of, oh, Hickson, was it, Hickman?

MRS. HITCHCOCK (*astonished and disturbed*). Ey, ey –

MUSGRAVE. What was it now, his name – Billy – Billy –

MRS. HITCHCOCK (*very upset*). Billy Hicks. Hicks. Aye, oh, strange, serjeant, strange roads bringing you along, I'd not wonder.

MUSGRAVE. What do you mean? . . . It *was* Hicks – I remember.

MRS. HITCHCOCK (*reminiscently*). Not what you'd call a bad young feller, you know – but he weren't no good neither. He'd come in here pissed of a Sat'dy night – I'd tell him straight out, 'You needn't reckon on to get any more here.' But he'd lean on this bar and he'd look at me, and he'd sing. You know – *hymns* – 'Uplift your heads, you gates of brass' – church hymns, he'd sing. Like he'd say to me, 'I'll sing for me drinking, missus' . . . hymns . . .

She hums the tune of 'Uplift your heads' and breaks off sharply.

He gave her a baby, and he went straight off to the war. Or the rebellions, they called it. They told us he was killed.

MUSGRAVE (*without emotion*). Aye, he was killed. He was shot dead last year . . . Gave a baby to who?

MRS. HITCHCOCK (*jerks her thumb to door behind bar*). Her.

MUSGRAVE (*truly surprised*). Go on?

MRS. HITCHCOCK. True. But when it wor born, it came a kind of bad shape, pale, sick: it wor dead and in the ground in no more nor two month. About the time they called him dead, y'see. What d'you reckon to that?

MUSGRAVE (*carelessly*). It's not material. He was no great friend to me. But maybe, as you said, strange. He did use to sing. And yellow hair he had, didn't he? (*He goes to the door behind the bar and calls.*) Have ye finished your dinners? Because we'll take a look at the town before it gets dark. (*Confidently to* MRS. HITCHCOCK) What you've just been telling me, don't tell it to these. Dead men and dead children should bide where they're put and not be rose up to the thoughts of the living. It's bad for discipline ... (*He calls again.*) Come on, let's be having you!

The SOLDIERS *come in.* MUSGRAVE *points to each one as they enter.*

East; south; west; I'll go north; I'm told it suits my nature. Then meet at the churchyard rail and tell me what you've seen. Let's make it sharp.

They go out.

SCENE THREE

The churchyard.

Sunset. HURST *enters and walks about, whistling nervously. The* SLOW COLLIER *enters and looks at him. They pass each other, giving each other good hard stares. The* SLOW COLLIER *is about to leave the stage when he turns round and calls.*

SLOW COLLIER. Hey! Soldier!

HURST. Aye?

SLOW COLLIER. How many on you is there?

HURST. Four.

SLOW COLLIER. Four . . . Four dead red rooks and be damned.

HURST. What? What's that?

SLOW COLLIER (*contemptuously*). Arrh . . .

He slouches out.

HURST *makes to follow, but decides not to, and continues walking about.*

MUSGRAVE *enters.*

MUSGRAVE. Coldest town I ever was in. What did you see?

HURST. Hardly a thing. Street empty, windows shut, two old wives on a doorstep go indoors the minute I come. Three men on one corner, two men on another, dirty looks and no words from any on 'em. There's one man swears a curse at me just now. That's all.

MUSGRAVE. H'm . . .

He calls to offstage.

Hello! We're over here!

ATTERCLIFFE *enters.*

What did you see?

ATTERCLIFFE. Hardly a thing. Street empty, doors locked, windows blind, shops cold and empty. A young lass calls her kids in from playing in the dirt—she sees me coming, so she calls 'em. There's someone throws a stone –

MUSGRAVE. A stone?

ATTERCLIFFE. Aye. I don't know who did it and it didn't hit me, but it was thrown.

HURST. It's a cold poor town, I'm telling you, serjeant.

MUSGRAVE. Coldest town I ever was in. And here's the fourth of us.

Enter SPARKY.

What did you see?

SPARKY. Hardly a thing. Street empty, no chimneys smoking, no horses, yesterday's horsedung frozen on the road. Three men at a corner-post, four men leaning on a wall. No words: but some chalked up on a closed door – they said: 'Soldiers go home'.

HURST. Go home?

SPARKY. That's it, boy: home. It's a place they think we have somewhere. And what did *you* see, serjeant?

MUSGRAVE. Nothing different from you . . . So, here is our town and here are we. All fit and appropriate.

HURST (*breaking out suddenly*). Appropriate? Serjeant, now we've come with you so far. And every day we're in great danger. We're on the run, in red uniforms, in a black-and-white coalfield; and it's cold; and the money's running out that you stole from the Company office; and we don't know who's heard of us or how much they've heard. Isn't it time you brought out clear just what you've got in mind?

MUSGRAVE (*ominously*). Aye? Is it? And any man else care to tell me what the time is?

ATTERCLIFFE (*reasonably*). Now serjeant, please, easy—we're all your men, and we agreed –

HURST. All right: if we *are* your men, we've rights.

MUSGRAVE (*savagely*). The only right *you* have is a rope around your throat and six foot six to drop from. On the run? Stolen money? I'm talking of a murdered officer, shot down in a street fight, shot down in one night's work. They put that to the rebels, but *I* know *you* were the man. We deserted, but you killed.

HURST. I'd a good reason . . .

MUSGRAVE. I know you had reason, else I'd not have left you alive to come with us. All I'm concerned about this minute is to tell you how you stand. And you stand in my power. But there's more to it than a bodily blackmail – isn't there? – because my power's the power of God, and that's what's brought me here and all three of you with me. You know my words and purposes – it's not just authority of the orderly room, it's not just three stripes, it's not just given to me by the reckoning of my mortal brain – well, *where* does it come from?

He flings this question fiercely at HURST.

HURST (*trying to avoid it*). All right, I'm not arguing –
MUSGRAVE. *Where!*
HURST (*frantically defensive*). I don't believe in God!
MUSGRAVE. You don't? Then what's this!

He jabs his thumb into HURST'S *cheek and appears to scrape something off it.*

HURST. Sweat.
MUSGRAVE. The coldest winter for I should think it's ten years, and the man sweats like a bird-bath!
HURST (*driven in a moral corner*). Well, why not, because –
MUSGRAVE (*relentless*). Go on – because?
HURST (*browbeaten into incoherence*). All right, because I'm afraid. 'Cos I thought when I met you, I thought we'd got the same motives. To get out, get shut o' the Army – with its 'treat-you-like-dirt-but-you-do-the-dirty-work' – 'kill *him*, kill *them*, they're all bloody rebels, State of Emergency, high standard of turnout, military bearin' – so *I* thought up some killing, I said I'll get me own in. I thought o' the Rights of Man. Rights o' the Rebels: that's *me*! Then I *went*. And here's a serjeant on the road, he's took two men, he's deserted same as me, he's got money, he can bribe a civvy skipper to carry us to England . . . It's nowt to do wi' *God*. I don't understand all that about God, why d'you bring God into it! You've come here to tell the people and then there'd be no more war –

MUSGRAVE (*taking him up with passionate affirmation*). Which *is* the word of God! Our message without God is a bad belch and a hiccup. You three of you, without me, are a bad belch and a hiccup. How d'you think you'd do it, if I wasn't here? Tell me, go on, tell me!

HURST (*still in his corner*). Why then I'd – I'd – I'd tell 'em, Sarnt Musgrave, I'd bloody stand, and tell 'em, and –

MUSGRAVE. Tell 'em *what*!

HURST (*made to appear more stupid than he really is*). All right: like, the war, the Army, colonial wars, we're treated like dirt, out there, and for to do the dirty work, and –

MUSGRAVE (*with withering scorn*). And they'd run you in and run you up afore the clock struck five! You don't understand about God! But you think, yourself, you, alone, stupid, without a gill of discipline, illiterate, ignorant of the Scriptures – you think you can make a whole town, a whole nation, understand the cruelty and greed of armies, what it means, and how to punish it! You hadn't even took the precaution to find the cash for your travel. I paid your fare!

HURST (*knuckling under*). All right. You paid . . . You're the Serjeant . . . All right. Tell us what to do.

MUSGRAVE (*the tension eased*). Then we'll sit down, and we'll be easy. It's cold atween these tombs, but its private. Sit down. Now: you can consider, and you can open your lugs and you can listen – ssh! Wait a minute . . .

The SLOW COLLIER *enters at one side, the* PUGNACIOUS *and* EARNEST COLLIERS *at the other. All three carry pick-hefts as clubs.*

SLOW COLLIER (*calls to the other two*). Four on 'em, you see. They're all here together.

PUGNACIOUS COLLIER. Setting in the graveyard, eh, like a coffin-load o' sick spooks.

EARNEST COLLIER (*coming towards the soldiers*). Which one's the Serjeant?

MUSGRAVE (*standing up*). Talk to me.

EARNEST COLLIER. Aye and I will too. There's a Union made at this colliery, and we're strong. When we say strike, we strike, all ends of us: that's fists, and it's pick-hefts and it's stones and it's feet. If you work in the coal-seam you carry iron on your clogs – see!

He thrusts up his foot menacingly.

PUGNACIOUS COLLIER. And you fight for your life when it's needed.

MUSGRAVE. So do some others of us.

EARNEST COLLIER. Ah, no, lobster, *you* fight for pay. You go sailing on what they call punitive expeditions, against what you call rebels, and you shoot men down in streets. But not here. These streets is *our* streets.

MUSGRAVE. Anything else?

EARNEST COLLIER. No. Not this evening. Just so as you know, that's all.

PUGNACIOUS COLLIER. Setting in the graveyard. Look at 'em, for Godsake. Waiting for a riot and then they'll have a murder. Why don't *we* have one *now*: it's dark enough, ent it?

EARNEST COLLIER. Shut up. It'll do when it's time. Just so as they know, that's all.

The COLLIERS *turn to go.*

MUSGRAVE. Wait a minute.

They pause.

Who told you we'd come to break the strike?

EARNEST COLLIER. Eh?

MUSGRAVE. Who told you?

EARNEST COLLIER. Nobody told us. We don't need to be told. You see a strike: you see soldiers: there's only one reason.

MUSGRAVE. Not this time there isn't. We haven't been sent for –

PUGNACIOUS COLLIER. Get away wi' that –

MUSGRAVE. And all soldiers aren't alike, you know. Some of us is human.

SLOW COLLIER } Arrh –
PUGNACIOUS COLLIER } (*laughs*)

MUSGRAVE. Now I'm in Mrs. Hitchcock's bar tonight until such time as she closes it. There'll be my money on the counter, and if you want to find what I'm doing here you can come along and see. I speak fair; you take it fair. Right?

EARNEST COLLIER. No it's not right, Johnny Clever. These streets is our streets, so you learn a warning . . . Come on, leave 'em be, *we* know what they're after. Come on . . .

The COLLIERS *go, growling threateningly.*

ATTERCLIFFE. They hate us, Serjeant, don't they? Wouldn't you say that's good?

MUSGRAVE. Because of the bad coal-trade they hate us; the rest just follows. True, there's one man talks of shooting rebels down in streets, but the others only think of bayonets turned on pitmen, and that's no good. At the present, they believe we've come to kill them. Soon they'll find we haven't, so they'll stop hating. Maybe even some o' them'll come and sign on. You'll see: His Worship's sovereigns – they'll fall too damned heavy into these boys' pockets. But we'll watch and take count, till we know the depth of the corruption. 'Cos all that we know now is that we've had to leave behind us a colonial war that is a war of sin and unjust blood.

ATTERCLIFFE (*sharply*). All wars is sin, serjeant . . .

MUSGRAVE (*impatient*). I'm not discussing that. Single purpose at a single time: your generalities aren't material: this is particular – one night's work in the streets of one city, and it damned all four of us and the war it was part of. We're each one guilty of particular blood. We've come to this town to work that guilt back to where it began.

He turns to SPARKY.

Why to this town? Say it, say it!

SPARKY (*as with a conditioned reflex*). Billy. Billy's dead. He wor my mucker, back end of the rear rank. He wor killed dead. He came from this town.

MUSGRAVE (*relentless*). Go on.

SPARKY (*appealing*). Serjeant –

MUSGRAVE. Use your clear brain, man, and tell me what you're doing here! Go on.

SPARKY (*incoherent with recollecting what he wants to forget*). I'm doing here? I'm doing . . . Serjeant, you know it. 'Cos he died. That wor Billy. I got drunk. Four days and four nights. After work of one night. Absent. Not sober. Improperly dressed.

He tries to turn it into one of his jokes.

Stick me in a cell, boys,
Pull the prison bell
Black Jack Musgrave
To call the prison roll –

Sarnt, no offence – 'First ye'll serve your punishment' he says. 'Then I'll show you how,' he says, the Serjeant. I says, 'You'll show me what?' He says, 'I'll show you how your Billy can be paid for.' . . . I didn't want to pay for him – what had I to care for a colonial war? . . .

He meets MUSGRAVE'S *eye and takes a grip on his motives.*

But I *did* want to pay for him, didn't I?' Cos that's why I'm here. 'You go down, I'll follow' . . . You, Serjeant, ent it?

Black Jack Musgrave
He always calls the roll.

He says:

Go down to Billy's town
Tell 'em how he died.

And that's what I'm doing here. The Serjeant pays the fare. Here I am, I'm paid for. Next turn's for Billy. Or all that's left of Billy. Who'll give me an offer for his bones? Sixpence for a bone, for a bone of my dead mucker . . .

He again avoids emotion by turning on HURST, *jeeringly.*

You didn't even know him when he lived, you weren't in his squad, what do *you* care that he's dead? To you he's like God, ent that the truth, you don't care and you're not bothered!

HURST (*angrily*). Hold your noise, you dirty turd! Who are you telling!

SPARKY. You. Oh you, me boy, you. A man and a soldier –

He meets MUSGRAVE'S *eye again, and his voice trails away.*

– a man and a soldier . . .

MUSGRAVE (*emphatically*). Aye. And *you're* a soldier. Don't forget that. You're my man and you'll hear me. You're not on any drunk now. Now you've got discipline. You've got grief, but good order, and its turned to the works of God!

SPARKY (*submissively*). Yes, Sarnt.

MUSGRAVE (*to* HURST). Turned to the works of God!

HURST (*submissively*). Yes, Sarnt.

MUSGRAVE (*in a more encouraging voice*). There was talk about danger. Well, I never heard of no danger yet that wasn't comparative. Compare it against your purposes. And compare it against my strategy. Remember: the roads are closed, the water's frozen, the telegraph wires are weighted down with snow, they haven't *built* the railway. We came here safe, and here we are, safe here. The winter's giving us one day, two days, three days even – that's clear safe for us to hold our time, take count of the corruption, then stand before this people with our white shining word, and let it dance! It's a hot coal, this town, despite that it's freezing – choose your minute and blow: and whoosh, she's flamed your roof off! They're trembling already into the strikers' riots. Well, their riots and our war are the same one corruption. This town is ours, it's ready for us: and its people, when they've heard us, and the Word of God, crying the murders that we've done – I'll tell you they'll turn to us, and they'll turn against that war!

ATTERCLIFFE (*gravely*). All wars, Serjeant Musgrave. They've got to turn against all wars. Colonial war, do we say, no war of honour? I'm a private soldier, I never had no honour, I went killing for the Queen, I did it for me wages, that wor my life. But I've got a new life. There was one night's work, and I said: no more killing.

HURST (*with excitement*). It's time we did our *own* killing.

ATTERCLIFFE. No, boy, it isn't.

HURST. Aye, and I mean it. We're all on the run, and we're all of us deserters. We're wild-wood mad and raging. We caught it overseas and now we've got to run around the English streets biting every leg to give it *them* – that can't be done without –

MUSGRAVE (*interrupting*). Listen to me!

HURST (*subsiding*). Serjeant.

MUSGRAVE (*with angry articulation*). We are here with a word. That's all. That's particular. Let the word dance. That's all that's material, this day and for the next. What happens afterwards, the Lord God will provide. I am with you, He said. Abide with Me in Power. A Pillar of Flame before the people. What we show here'll lead forward forever, against dishonour, and greed, and murder-for-greed! There is our duty, the new, deserter's duty: God's dance on this earth: and all that we are is His four strong legs to dance it . . . Very well. That'll do. It's dark. We'll go in. Now we'll be likely buying drinks around and so on, in the public tonight.

I don't want to see any o' you with more nor you can hold. When there's danger, there's temptation. So keep it gay, but that's all. Off you go now! Take 'em in.

ATTERCLIFFE (*as the senior*). All right then, smartly now, walking up the street. Remember, we're recruiting. I'll give you the time – left right left right.

They walk out briskly, leaving MUSGRAVE *alone. As they go, the* BARGEE *enters, and gives them a parody salute in passing.* MUSGRAVE *doesn't see him, walks downstage, crosses his hands on his chest and stands to pray. The* BARGEE *parodies his attitude behind his back.*

MUSGRAVE. God, my Lord God. Have You or have You not delivered this town into my hands? All my life a soldier I've made You prayers and made them straight, I've reared my one true axe against the timber and I've launched it true. My regiment was my duty, and I called Death honest, killing by the book – but it all got scrawled and mucked about and I could not think clear . . . Now I have my duties different. I'm in this town to change all soldiers' duties. My prayer is: keep my mind clear so I can weigh Judgement against the Mercy and Judgement against the Blood, and make this Dance as terrible as You have put it into my brain. The Word alone is terrible: the Deed must be worse. But I know it is Your Logic, and You will provide.

He pauses for a moment, then turns sharply on his heel and strides away after the soldiers. He still fails to see the BARGEE. *The latter has whipped off his hat at the conclusion of* MUSGRAVE'S *prayer, and now he stands looking solemnly up to Heaven. He gives a sanctimonious smirk and breathes: 'Amen'.*

Act Two

SCENE ONE

The bar of the public house.

A scene of noise and conviviality, crowded confusion. MRS. HITCHCOCK *is seated behind the bar, drinking tea with brandy in it.* ANNIE *is going backwards and forwards in the room carrying drinks and empties.* MUSGRAVE *is sitting with a tankard, calmly watching.* SPARKY *is wearing his drum and alternately beating it and drinking and singing. The* SLOW *and* PUGNACIOUS COLLIERS, *well-oiled, are drinking and dancing. The* BARGEE *is drinking and dancing and playing a mouth-organ and beating time to the singing.* ATTERCLIFFE *is drinking and dancing and pinning cockades to the hats of the* COLLIERS. *At intervals one of the dancers grabs hold of* ANNIE *and swirls her around, but she retains a contemptuous aloofness and carries on with her work. As the scene opens the men (save* MUSGRAVE*) are all joining in the chorus:*

CHORUS. Blow your morning bugles
Blow your calls ey-ho
Form platoon and dress the ranks
And blow, boys blow!

This chorus is sung (with progressively less correctness) by most of the men at the end of each verse of the song.

SPARKY (*singing*).

When first I came to the barracks
My heart it grieved full sore
For leaving of my old true love
That I would see no more.

chorus

SLOW COLLIER (*to* MUSGRAVE, *who is studying a notebook*). I'm not signing nowt. Provisional, I said, provisional.

MUSGRAVE. Aye, aye, provisional. No one makes it different.

SPARKY (*sings*).

They made us drill and muster
And stand our sentries round
And I never thought I'd lay again
A girl upon the ground.

chorus

PUGNACIOUS COLLIER (*to* ATTERCLIFFE). That's *my* point, *my* point, too . . . all right enlisting, aye . . . but I'm a married man –

SPARKY (*sings*).

But soon we were paraded
And marching to the war
And in every town the girls lay down
And cried out loud for more.

chorus

PUGNACIOUS COLLIER (*to* ATTERCLIFFE). I'm not so sure I like your looks, aye, *you*!

SPARKY. Me?

PUGNACIOUS COLLIER (*pointing to* ATTERCLIFFE). You!

SPARKY (*sings*).

And when we'd lodge in billets
We'd beer in every can
And the landlord's wife and daughters learnt
Just how to love a man.

chorus

PUGNACIOUS COLLIER (*going at* SPARKY). I'm a married man, bedamn, I've got a wife, I've got a wife, a wife . . .

SPARKY. No one's taking her from you.

PUGNACIOUS COLLIER. Not you?

SPARKY. No.

MUSGRAVE (*interrupting*). All right, steady, friend, *no one*.

SLOW COLLIER. *I'll* take her from you when you go to the war, I'll take her –

PUGNACIOUS COLLIER. You?

SLOW COLLIER. Me! Or no, no, no: I'll make do with our Annie!

He makes a drunken lurch at her which she more or less evades.

Come on then, mucker!

Foiled by ANNIE, *he seizes the* PUGNACIOUS COLLIER *and they do a clog dance together while the* BARGEE *plays. Chorus while they dance, and general cheer.*

BARGEE. Bring 'em in some more, Annie, it's all on the Queen tonight – how many have you listed, serjeant!

MUSGRAVE. I'm not listing no one tonight. (*He bangs with his tankard for silence*). Now then, boys, everybody –

BARGEE (*officiously*). Everybody listen!

A roll on the drum.

BARGEE. Listen!

MUSGRAVE (*expansively*). This is Her Majesty's hospitality – that's *all* that it is, boys, on a soldier's honour, so! Any man that drinks tonight –

BARGEE. Any man that drinks tonight –

MUSGRAVE. He drinks at the Queen's pleasure, and none of you need fear to find a shilling in your mug at end of it – that like o' lark's finished and gone with the old days – the Army only wants good men, that's free men, of your own true will for the Empire – so drink and welcome: and all men in this town –

BARGEE. All men in this town –

MUSGRAVE. When we hold our meeting and the drum beats and we bring out our colours, then you can make your return in the signing of your names – but only those men willing! That's all : drink and away!

A roll on the drum.

BARGEE. Drink and away, me boys, hurray!

PUGNACIOUS COLLIER. Serjeant, you're a bleeding lobster, but you're a man! Shake me by the hand!

The BARGEE *gives a whoop and starts to dance, playing a mouth-organ. He stumbles, and everybody laughs.*

ANNIE (*scornfully*). And what regiment's *that* one, serjeant? The Backwards-Mounted-Foot?

BARGEE. I'll tell you, me lovely, why not? The Queen's Own Randy Chancers : or the Royal Facing-Both-Ways – hey, me clever monkeys :

> Old Joe looks out for Joe
> Plots and plans and who lies low?
> But the Lord provides, says Crooked Old Joe.

MUSGRAVE (*looking sharply at him*). Eh?

The BARGEE *shrugs and grins.* MUSGRAVE *dismisses the question.*

BARGEE. Just a little joke . . . little joke : little dog, I'll be with you . . .

He whistles 'Michael Finnegan' and ducks out of the pub. Meanwhile SPARKY *has taken off his drum and come downstage to intercept* ANNIE. ATTERCLIFFE *is drinking with the* COLLIERS *and one or other of these plays the drum at intervals. The going of the* BARGEE *has made the room somewhat quieter for a while.*

SPARKY (*to* ANNIE). Little dog – bow-wow, *I'm* a little dog, any trick for a bit of biscuit, Annie, bit o' meat – look :

He takes a pack of cards out of his pocket and presents it.

Take one, go on, take one.

She obeys.

Well?

ANNIE. Queen o' Spades.

SPARKY (*laughing*). That's a hell of a card to take: I think there's treacle on it, sticks to all fingers out o' this pack, I call her Grandma, makes her gentle, y'see – hope she'll kiss me whiskers and leave it at that.

He has replaced the card and shuffles.

Now then, take first four cards on top. Tell me what they are.

ANNIE (*obeying*). Eight Nine Ten Jack, all spades.

SPARKY (*triumphantly*). Right, right, calls the roll straight up to the one you took, the Queen, and where's the one you took? On the bottom – take it!

ANNIE (*obeying*). It is the Queen and all!

SPARKY. 'Course it is: I *told* you. That's what I call life – it all turns up in the expected order, but not when you expect it. And that's what sets your two teeth laughing, click-clack, doesn't it, ha ha ha! Oh I'm a clever lad, you see, they call me Sparky, lots o' games, lots o' jokes . . .

ANNIE (*not impressed*). Lots of liquor too. Now get out of me road while I fetch some more – *I've* got *work*, you know.

SPARKY (*going after her and again intercepting her*). Hey, but lovey, listen: there was an Englishman, a Welshman and a bloody great Irish – all three of 'em on Defaulters, y'see, for drunk. Now the Orderly Sarnt, he says, 'One, Two, Three, all we want's a Scotchman.' And a voice in the guardroom-yard says: 'Hoots awa', man, I'm taking back the empties fairst.'

She avoids him and goes away to the bar, thus ruining the

climax of his tale. He tries to follow her up, but this time he is intercepted by MUSGRAVE. HURST *appears in the doorway.* ANNIE *looks up at him and follows him with her eyes for the rest of this dialogue.*

MUSGRAVE (*to* SPARKY). You've had enough.

SPARKY. I'm not drunk.

MUSGRAVE. No and you won't be neither. This is no time.

SPARKY (*pointing to* HURST). No – and *here* he comes, look at him.

MUSGRAVE (*striding angrily over to* HURST). Where have you been?

HURST (*surlily*). Down by the canal.

MUSGRAVE. Why?

HURST. All right, I'd got things on my mind. And I'll tell you this, Serjeant, it isn't enough.

MUSGRAVE. What isn't enough?

HURST. What you and that old cuckold are reckoning to do. It's all soft, it's all flat, it's all – God and the Word! Tchah! What good's a word, what good's a bloody word, they can *all* talk bloody words – it isn't enough: we've got to be strong!

MUSGRAVE. Leave it alone, boy. *I* hold the logic. *You* hold some beer and get on with your work.

MUSGRAVE *walks away from* HURST.

HURST (*shouts after him*). It isn't enough!

He turns to find ANNIE *standing at his elbow, looking into his face and handing him a tankard of beer. He takes it and drinks it rapidly, without looking at her.*

MRS. HITCHCOCK (*calling from the bar*). The Queen's in debt, Serjeant!

MUSGRAVE. Hello, ma'am?

MRS. HITCHCOCK. I said the Queen's in debt!

MUSGRAVE. Chalk it up Ma'am, and another round for us all.

MRS. HITCHCOCK. No more chalk.

MUSGRAVE. Easily found though.

He plunges his hand in his pocket and pulls out a quantity of money. He does a rapid count, whistles in consternation, and selects a few coins.

ATTERCLIFFE (*watching him*). Not so much of it left, is there?

MUSGRAVE. Easy, easy.

He goes over to the bar and pays. SPARKY *is now showing his card tricks to the* COLLIERS. ANNIE *plucks at the sleeve of the pensive* HURST.

ANNIE (*simply*). You're the best to look at of all the four, aren't you?

HURST. Eh? What's that?

ANNIE. Tell you again? Why? You know it, don't you?

HURST (*preoccupied*). I'd forgot it. I'd other matter beyond wondering what you'd think to our looks.

He studies her closer, and snaps out of his gloomy mood into an attitude of lady-killing arrogance.

Why, I don't need to think o' women. I let them think of *me*. I've knocked greasier ones than you between me porridge and me bacon. Don't flatter yourself.

ANNIE. I'm not, soldier: I'm flattering you. I'll come to you tonight.

HURST (*pleased, though trying not to show it*). Will you? That's a good choice, you've got sense.

ANNIE (*meaningly*). But you forget them other matters, eh?

HURST (*decidedly warming to her*). I'll try . . . I'd rather. I hope I can . . . Stand straight: let's see . . . Gay and greasy, like I like 'em! You're big, and you're bonny. A good shape, I'd call it. And you've got good hair, but wants a comb in it. You ought to wash your face. And your neck smells of soot, don't it?

ANNIE (*accepting this in the spirit in which it's meant*). I've been blowing up the fire.

HURST (*boastfully*). Ah, the last I had was a major's daughter. I've got standards. Lovely.

ATTERCLIFFE *comes across to them.*

ATTERCLIFFE. You said he was the best looker. I heard you. But it's not true.

ANNIE. Then who is? You?

ATTERCLIFFE. I'll tell you a tale about that. That pitman over there – he said to me he thought I'd steal his wife. By God, I'd sooner steal his nightsoil . . . I've got a wife. Ask me to tell you one o' these days.– Sparky'd make a joke of it – wouldn't you, Sparky!

The last phrases are shouted across the room.

SPARKY (*shouts back*). Not any more – we're all going too fast.

He turns back to the COLLIERS

Down, down – any card, any card, mate – tell me its name – down.

PUGNACIOUS COLLIER. Six o' Hearts!

SPARKY. Right, right – *and* we shuffle and cut –

Enter the BARGEE.

BARGEE (*shouts*). Time, gennelmen please, everybody time, last orders everybody!

MRS. HITCHCOCK (*angrily*). Who's given *you* leave to do the calling here!

BARGEE (*singing*).

Blow your morning bugles
Blow your calls ey-ho –

If it's not me and it's not you, there'll be somebody else – *look*!

Enter CONSTABLE.

CONSTABLE. All right, Mrs. Hitchcock, it's time you closed your bar.

MRS. HITCHCOCK. What are you talking about!

CONSTABLE. Magistrates' orders, missus. All public houses to close at nine o'clock sharp, pending settlement of colliery dispute.

MRS. HITCHCOCK. It's the first I've heard of it.

SLOW COLLIER (*to the* CONSTABLE). Get out of it.

PUGNACIOUS COLLIER (*ditto*). Go home, you closhy bluebottle, and sweep your bloody chimney.

CONSTABLE. That'll do there.

MUSGRAVE. That'll do, lads, keep it easy.

PUGNACIOUS COLLIER (*to* MUSGRAVE). We're not in the Army yet, y'know!

ATTERCLIFFE. Steady, matey, steady. All friends, y'know: married men together.

PUGNACIOUS COLLIER. But, Serjeant, you're a man, and I'll *shake* you by the hand.

CONSTABLE (*now things seem quiet again.*). Magistrates issued the order only this evening, missus. I've let you stay open a lot longer than the others – it's nigh on a quarter to ten already – and I'm in my rights to allow an exception for this house, on account of the Army. Question of facilities. I trust you've made good use of the extra time, Sarnt Musgrave?

MUSGRAVE. H'm.

PUGNACIOUS COLLIER (*with great friendliness*). Have the last drink on me, bluebottle!

CONSTABLE (*curtly*). The last drink's been had already. Close your bar, please, missus.

PUGNACIOUS COLLIER (*an angry idea occurring to him*). Wait a minute . . . Suppose I join your Army. Suppose I bloody 'list. What does my wife do?

BARGEE. Cock-a-doodle-do!

PUGNACIOUS COLLIER (*finding his own answer*). She goes to bed with the Peeler! I'll break his wooden head off.

He goes for the CONSTABLE *with a tankard, the* CONSTABLE *staggers backwards and falls, the* COLLIER *raises his tankard to smash it into his face.* ATTERCLIFFE *and* MUSGRAVE, *being nearest, jump to prevent him.*

ATTERCLIFFE (*pulling the* COLLIER *fiercely back*). Hey, ey, ey, ey-ey, hold it there, boy, hold it there! My God, you might ha' killed him. No...

ATTERCLIFFE *is trembling all over.*

SLOW COLLIER. Why shouldn't he if he wants to?

ATTERCLIFFE (*with great passion*). We've had enough o' that already – no more, no more, no more of it.

MUSGRAVE (*holding* ATTERCLIFFE *to quiet him*). Stop it there!

CONSTABLE (*getting up slowly*). Stand back, stand back. By God, it's *time* this place was closed. Turn out into the street, go on with you, get home. D'ye want me to whistle up me specials? Go on.

He hurls the COLLIERS *and* BARGEE *out of the pub.*

ATTERCLIFFE. He was going to, Serjeant. He would have, he'd have killed him. It's always here. Kill him. Kill.

MUSGRAVE (*roughly*). That'll do... We've all had enough, Mr. Constable. I'll get this lot to bed.

CONSTABLE. All right then. And try and keep folk quiet. I know you've got to buy 'em drink and that – but... *you* know – easy?

MUSGRAVE. Aye aye, easy. We know the trends. Don't you worry: *we* stand for law-and-order too, don't we?

CONSTABLE. Well, I hope so –

He goes to the door and calls into the street.

I said home, no loitering, go on, go on, or I'll run you in!

He comes back to MUSGRAVE *in a confidential conspiratorial sort of way.*

It's a sort of curfew, you see. I told His Worship: 'If there's trouble at night, you can't hold *me* responsible. I've done my best,' I said – I told him frank . . . Oh, and while we're on about His Worship, Serjeant, I might as well take occasion to discuss some names with you. There's a few like I could tell you as'd look very convenient on a regimental muster.

MUSGRAVE (*coldly*). I'm here for volunteers only, you know.

CONSTABLE (*insinuatingly*). Ah well, what's a volunteer? You, you, and you – the old Army custom – eh, Serjeant? Mrs. Hitchcock! A couple o' pints o' taddy for me and the Serjeant.

MRS. HITCHCOCK. We're closed.

CONSTABLE (*broad-mindedly*). That's all right, missus. Serve to the Serjeant: hotel-resident. All above the board.

MRS. HITCHCOCK (*to* ANNIE). So take 'em their drinks. Queen as pays.

She pours herself out another cup of tea. ANNIE *prepares the drinks and brings them to* MUSGRAVE *and the* CONSTABLE, *who gets into a huddle over a list the latter produces.*

SPARKY (*to the other two* SOLDIERS). Very commodious Queen. I say, a very commodious Queen, ha ha, if she'd drank all she paid for tonight, heh, Sponge By Appointment, they could swab out the Windsor Castle Guardhouse, ha ha, who'd be a Coldstream! I say, they could swab out –

ATTERCLIFFE. Oh shut up, man, for God's sake. We've had all we can take of your stinking patter.

SPARKY (*aggrieved*). Ey-ey, matey – ey-ey.

He withdraws, hurt.

HURST (*to* ATTERCLIFFE). Shut up yourself – what's got into you?

ATTERCLIFFE. Why, *you* were making enough carry-on earlier, weren't you? Are you so daft or so drunk you didn't see what just happened?

HURST. There was nowt happened. Couple o' pitmen three parts pissed? What's the matter wi' that? You were near as bad yourself – don't tell *me*. *You* were on about your *wife!*

ATTERCLIFFE. There was all but a man killed. We've come to stop it, not to start it – go on, sing to us.

He sings, with savage emphasis.

> Who'll give a penny to the poor blind man
> Holds out his hand with an old tin can.

– 'Cos that's all you are and it curdles up my bowels. I'm going to the coach-house.

HURST. The coach-house! What for?

ATTERCLIFFE. Where there's a man to talk to who don't talk like a fool.

He goes out of the door behind the bar.

SPARKY. Here, what d'you think to *him*? What sort o' talk does he reckon he'll get.

HURST. Keep your mind off that!

SPARKY (*wildly*). Rattling, clattering, old bones in a box? Billy used to sing, d'you think he'll have a sing-song?

HURST. I don't understand you. This don't make *me* laugh. It fair makes me sick.

SPARKY (*jeeringly*). Sick and bloody scared. Hey-ey, that's you, that's you truly.

HURST. Well, I've got things on my mind. If you can call it scared –

SPARKY. You and me, we're a pair, boy.

HURST (*savagely*). All right. But you'll learn. All *right*.

He turns abruptly away, and broods.

SPARKY (*beckoning* ANNIE, *who comes unenthusiastically*). I say, Annie – oh I'll tell you what, Annie, I don't know what I'm doing here.

She looks at him questioningly; he waves the point aside.

Aha, for that . . . Look, we've made us our beds up in the stables – ha, loose-box for every man, but the serjeant in the house.

ANNIE. Aye, I know.

SPARKY. We call it the Discipline, y'see. Yes-sarnt-no-sarnt, three-bags-full-sarnt – that's our merry lives. Ha ha. Third box from the end tonight, the fastest racehorse of 'em all. Oaks, Derby, I carry 'em away, boy: but I'm best at a steeple-chase – *hup* and *hover*, hedge and ditch, dear, and not by soldiers' numbers neither . . . Come for a gallop.

It is clear from the tone of the last phrase he is not joking.

ANNIE (*unemotionally*). Not tonight.

SPARKY. Oh . . . Go on, tonight.

ANNIE (*with something of a sneer*). Maybe next I will. I can't tell from day to day.

SPARKY. No more can I. You know, you've not yet give me one little laugh . . . But I'll contrive it: now y'see, there was a butcher, a baker, and a cats'-meat-man, all on the edge of the river. And down this river comes this dead dog, floating.

HURST (*whose head has dropped, suddenly jerks himself up again*). God, I was near asleep! I started a bad dream and it woke me.

MUSGRAVE (*to the* CONSTABLE). No, mister, it won't wash. We can't play pressgangs these days. If a man gets drunk and then signs, all right: but otherwise –

CONSTABLE (*vexed*). You're not over-co-operative, are you?

MUSGRAVE. I'm sorry. Oh, I'll see what I can do: but I won't promise more. Besides, agitators is agitators, in or out the Army. I'm not sure we want 'em. But I'll think. Good night.

He goes with the CONSTABLE *to the street door.*

CONSTABLE. Good night. Good night, missus.

Exit the CONSTABLE. MUSGRAVE *comes down to the* SOLDIERS.

MUSGRAVE (*calling* ANNIE). Lassie.

ANNIE. Hello.

MUSGRAVE. These are my men. They're here with their work to do. You will not distract them.

ANNIE. I won't?

MUSGRAVE. No. Because *they* know, whether you know it or not, that there's work is for women and there's work is for men: and let the two get mixed, you've anarchy.

ANNIE (*rather taken aback*). Oh? And what's anarchy? You, you clever grinder – words and three stripes –

MUSGRAVE. Look, lassie, anarchy: now, we're soldiers. Our work isn't easy, no and it's not soft: it's got a strong name – duty. And it's drawn out straight and black for us, a clear plan. But if you come to us with what you call your life or love – *I'd* call it your indulgence – and you scribble all over that plan, you make it crooked, dirty, idle, untidy, *bad* – there's anarchy. I'm a religious man. I know words, and I know deeds, and I know how to be strong. So do these men. You will not stand between them and their strength! Go on now: take yourself off.

ANNIE. A little bit of wind and a little bit of water –

MRS. HITCHCOCK. Annie –

ANNIE. But it drowned three score of sailors, and the King of Norway's daughter. (*She smiles for the first time in the play.*)

She sings:

O mother O mother
It hurts me so sore
Sing dody-eye-dodo
Then ye daft little bitch

Ye should do it no more
For you've never left off
Since we sailed from the shore.

MRS. HITCHCOCK (*sharply*). Annie, get to bed.

MUSGRAVE (*to the* SOLDIERS). You two, get to bed. And pay heed to what I say.

ANNIE *goes out behind the bar, with a satirical curtsy.* MUSGRAVE *goes out by the street door.* HURST *makes a move as though to speak to him, but is too late. He stands reflective.*

SPARKY.

To bed to bed says Sleepy-head
Tarry a while says Slow
Open the book, says the wise old Rook
We'll have prayers before we go.

He sways a little tipsily, and laughs.

SCENE TWO

A street. Night.

The PUGNACIOUS *and* SLOW COLLIERS *enter, drunk and marching, the* BARGEE *drilling them. (This is a kind of 'Fred Karno' sequence which must be kept completely under control. At each command each of the three carries out, smartly, a drill-movement; but each drill movement is different for each man, and none of them performs the movement shouted. They must not be so drunk that they cannot appear erect and alertly jerking. The effect should be, not so much of three incompetents pretending to be soldiers, but of three trained soldiers gone mad.) The* COLLIERS *carry pickhefts as rifles, and the* BARGEE *an oar.*
MUSGRAVE *enters, and stands quietly watching.*

BARGEE. Right turn. Forward march. Left right left right left right left.

PUGNACIOUS COLLIER. To the front present. Halt.

BARGEE. About turn.

SLOW COLLIER. One two three four.

BARGEE. Order arms.

PUGNACIOUS COLLIER. Present and correct. By the right, number.

SLOW COLLIER. One two three four.

They are now at attention, together.

PUGNACIOUS COLLIER. Present and correct.

BARGEE (*this order is properly obeyed*). Stand-at-ease. Easy . . .

PUGNACIOUS COLLIER (*breaking the spell*). I'll tell you what, we're bloody good.

BARGEE (*with enthusiasm*). Eh. Lordy, mucker – good! By, I've never seen the like – y'know, if you signed on they'd excuse you three weeks' drill on the spot. You make that serjeant look like Old-Mother-Bunch-in-the-Popshop, alongside o' you – love you, mucker, you're *born* to it!

PUGNACIOUS COLLIER. Well, why didn't I think on it afore?

SLOW COLLIER (*still on parade*). One two three four.

PUGNACIOUS COLLIER. I'd not ha' got wed if I'd known!

SLOW COLLIER (*suddenly coming to attention and starting off*). Quick march. One two three –

He bumps against WALSH, *who has just entered.*

Arh and be damned.

WALSH. Where the hell are you going to?

MUSGRAVE *starts to go out. He passes* WALSH, *who stops him with a hand on his chest.*

WALSH. So we was mistook, eh? You're not here for no riots after all, but catching up men: that's it, in'it? Guineas?

MUSGRAVE. Sovereigns.

PUGNACIOUS COLLIER (*suddenly indicating* MUSGRAVE *to* WALSH). Here. This one: three stripes, but he's a man.

WALSH. Aye? And what are you? Drunk on *his* money: marching and drilling like a pack o' nit-headed kids at a barrack-gate!

PUGNACIOUS COLLIER. Better nor bloody starve for no coal-owners, any road!

WALSH (*with passion*). I'll tell you, I'm that ashamed, I could spew.

MUSGRAVE (*gripping* WALSH *by the lapel and drawing him away*). Now listen here. I can see you, and see *you* what you are. I wasn't given these – (*he touches his stripes*) – for not knowing men from ninepins. Now I'm telling you one word and I'm telling you two, and that's all. (*He lowers his voice.*) You and me is brothers –

WALSH (*in high irony*). Eh begod! A Radical Socialist! Careful, soldier, careful. D'ye want to be hanged?

MUSGRAVE (*very seriously*). No jokes. I mean this. I mean it. Brothers in God –

WALSH (*even more scornful*). Oh, hoho, *that* –

MUSGRAVE. – And brothers in truth. So watch. And wait. I said, *wait*.

WALSH (*jeering*). Brothers in God.

Gentle Jesus send us rest
Surely the bosses knows what's best!

Get along with yer –

MUSGRAVE (*calmly*). Well: I said, wait. You'll see.

Exit MUSGRAVE.

SLOW COLLIER (*who has been marking time since his collision, now mutters*).

One two three four
Where's the man as lives next door?
Five six seven eight
Come on in, he's working late.

WALSH (*looking at him in disgust*). Holy God, I'd never ha' dreamt it.

SLOW COLLIER (*his muttering rising in volume*).

> Nine ten eleven twelve
> Take his place and help yourself,
> Thirteen fourteen fifteen sixteen –

PUGNACIOUS COLLIER (*with a stupid laugh*). He's talking about my wife.

SLOW COLLIER (*annoyed at being interrupted*).

> Thirteen fourteen fifteen sixteen
> Into the bed and there we'll fix him!

PUGNACIOUS COLLIER (*in rising rage*). I couldn't do it to the soldiers, I couldn't do it to the Peeler, but by, I'll do it to you! I'll break your bloody head.

He goes for SLOW COLLIER, *who hits him in the belly, lets off a yell and runs out.* PUGNACIOUS COLLIER *follows with a roar.*

BARGEE (*calling after them in glee*). Watch out for the Constable! Heh heh heh.

WALSH. Holy God! My mates! My brothers!

BARGEE (*kindly*). Ah well, they're drunk.

WALSH. I know they're drunk, and I know who's helped 'em to it.

BARGEE. I could help *you* to summat, and all.

WALSH. What's that?

BARGEE. They won't stay drunk all week. Oh the soldiers gives 'em sport, they *need* a bit o' sport, cold, hungry . . . When you want 'em, they'll be there. Crooked Joe, he's *here*.

WALSH. Aye?

BARGEE. Could you shoot a Gatling gun?

WALSH (*looking at him sideways*). I don't know.

BARGEE. If you really want a riot, why don't you go at it

proper? Come on, I'll tell you . . . (*He hops out, whistling 'Michael Finnegan' and looking back invitingly.*)

WALSH (*considering*). Aye, aye? Crooked, clever, keelman, eh? . . . Well – all right – then *tell* me!

He hurries after him.

SCENE THREE

Interior of the pub (stable and bedroom).

Night. The stage is divided into two distinct acting-areas. The downstage area represents the stable, and is supposed to be divided into three loose boxes. If it is not practicable for the partitions between these to be built, it should be sufficient to suggest them by the three mattresses which are laid parallel, feet to the audience. The actors must not appear to be able to see each other from box to box. The forestage represents the central passage of the stable and is the only access to the boxes. Entry to the forestage can be from both wings (one side leads to the house, the other to the yard and coach-house).

The upstage area, raised up at least a couple of feet, represents a bedroom in the house. It is only large enough to contain a brass-knobbed bedstead with a small table or other support for a candle. The two areas must be treated as completely separate. Access to the bedroom area should be from the rear, and the audience must not be allowed to think that the actors can see from one area to the other (except as regards the light in the window, which is supposed to be seen as if from across the yard).

MUSGRAVE, *in shirt and trousers, is sitting on the bed, reading by candlelight. His tunic etc. lies folded beside the bed.*

HURST *and* SPARKY *come into the stable from the house carrying palliasses and blankets. They proceed to make up their beds (in the two end boxes, leaving the middle one empty.* SPARKY *is at the house end,* HURST *next to the yard). They also undress to their shirts (of grey flannel) and their (long woollen) underpants and socks. Their clothes are laid out neatly beside the beds.*

SPARKY (*as he prepares for bed*). I say . . . I say, can you hear me?

HURST (*uninterested*). I can.

SPARKY. You know, I'll tell you: I'm a bit pissed tonight.

HURST. Uh. What of it?

SPARKY. What's that?

HURST. I said what of it? We all are, aren't we? *I* want an hour or two's sleep, I don't know about *you,* so let's have less o' your gab.

SPARKY. I say, there's a light on still in Black Jack's window.

HURST grunts.

MUSGRAVE *has now lain down on top of his blanket, but has not taken off his trousers, or put out his candle.*

SPARKY. Aye, aye. God's awake. Ha, Ha! Not only God neither. Y'know, I think there might be some of us mortal, even yet . . . I said God's awake!

HURST. I *heard* you, and be damned.

A pause.

SPARKY. Hour or two's sleep . . . What do you want to *sleep* for, and a fine fat tart all promised and ready!

HURST (*who has got undressed and under his blanket*). That'll do. Now shut your row, can't ye, when you're asked! I said I wanted to sleep, so let me.

SPARKY. Why, it's you she's promised, y'see – *you,* not me – wake up, mucker, wake up. She'll soon be here, y'see. She'll soon be here! (*He blows 'reveille' with his lips, then gets under his blanket.*) You, boy, *you,* not me! . . . Shall I sing you a song?

HURST (*almost asleep, and woken again*). Eh, what? Are you going to shut up, or aren't you!

SPARKY. Well, are *you* going to shut up or aren't you, when she comes? It's all right the best-looker loving the girl, but his two mates along the row wi' nowt but a bit o' wainscot atween – hey-ey-ey, it'll be agony for *us* tonight, y'know – so keep it quiet.

A pause.

(*He starts to sing, softly*).

She came to me at midnight
With the moonshine on her arms
And I told her not to make no noise
Nor cause no wild alarms.
But her savage husband he awoke
And up the stairs did climb
To catch her in her very deed:
So fell my fatal crime . . .

While he is singing, ANNIE *enters from the house, carrying a candle. She goes gently to* HURST'S *box and stands looking down at him. When she speaks, he sticks his head out of the bedclothes and looks at her.*
In the bedroom, MUSGRAVE *sits up, blows out his light, and goes to sleep.*

ANNIE (*with tender humour*). Here I come. Hello. I'm cold. I'm a blue ghost come to haunt you. Brr. Come on, boy, warm me up. You'll not catch cold off *me.*
HURST (*getting up*). No . . . I daresay not . . .

They put their arms round each other.

But what about the morning?
ANNIE. Ah, the morning's different, ent it? I'll not say nowt about mornings, 'cos then we'll *all* be cold. Cold and alone. Like, stand in a crowd but every one alone. One thousand men makes a regiment, you'd say?
HURST. Near enough.

ANNIE. But for all that, when you're with them, you're still alone. Ent that right? So huggle me into the warm, boy, now. Keep out the wind. It's late. Dark.

HURST (*suddenly breaking away from her*). No, I won't. I don't care what I said afore, it's all done, ended, capped – get away. Go on. Leave me be.

ANNIE (*astonished and hurt*). What is it? What's the matter? Lovey –

HURST (*with violence*). Go on. As far as *my* mind goes, it's morning already. Every one alone – that's all. You want me to lose my life inside of you –

ANNIE. No. No. But just for five hours, boy, six –

HURST. You heard Black Jack say what's right. Straight, clear, dark strokes, no scrawling, I was wrong afore, I didn't trust him. He talked about God, so I thought he wor just nowt. But what he said about *you*: there, that was truth. He's going to be *strong!*

ANNIE (*scornfully*). So *you* take note of Black Jack, do you?

HURST. Aye, and I do. It's too late tonight for anything else. He's got to be trusted, got to be strong, we've got no alternative!

ANNIE (*standing a little away from him*). My Christ then, they *have* found him a brother! It was only this evening, warn't it, *I* saw you, down by the canal, all alone and wretched –

She sings with fierce emphasis:

All round his hat he wore the green willow – !

HURST. All right.

ANNIE (*not letting him off*). But it can't have been you, can it? 'Cos now you're just the same as the rest of 'em – the Hungry Army! You eat and you drink and you go. Though *you* won't even eat when it's offered, will you? So *sprawl* yourself on the straw without me, get up to your work tomorrow, drum 'em in and write 'em down, infect 'em all and bury 'em! I don't care.

HURST. What are you on about, what's the matter, why don't you go when you're told? Godsake, Godsake, leave a man to his sleep!

ANNIE. You know what they call me?

HURST. I'd call you a bloody whoor –

ANNIE (*savagely ironical*). Oh, not just a whoor – *I'm* a whoor-to-the-soldiers – it's a class by itself.

ATTERCLIFFE *has entered from the yard with his bedding. They do not notice him yet.* ANNIE *turns to pleading again.*

ANNIE. Christ, let me stay with you. He called me life and love, boy, just you think on *that* a little.

HURST *pushes her away with a cry. She falls against* ATTERCLIFFE.

ATTERCLIFFE (*holding her up*). Life and love, is it? I'm an old soldier, girly, a dirty old bastard, me, and *I've* seen it all. Here.

He grips her and kisses her violently all over face and neck. He sneers at HURST.

Hey-up there, son, get in your manger and sleep, and leave this to the men.

HURST. All right . . . and you're welcome.

He goes to his box and lies down again, huffily, trying to sleep.

ATTERCLIFFE (*still holding* ANNIE, *with a sort of tenderness*). Now then, what'll I do to you, eh? How d'you reckon you're going to quench *me*? Good strong girly with a heart like a horsecollar, open it up and let 'em all in. And it still wouldn't do no good.

ANNIE (*hard and hostile*). Wouldn't it? Try.

ATTERCLIFFE. Ah, no. Not tonight. What would *you* know of soldiers?

ANNIE. More'n you'd think I'd know, maybe.

ATTERCLIFFE. I doubt it. Our Black Jack'd say it's not material. He'd say there's blood on these two hands. (*He looks at his hands with distaste.*) You can wipe 'em as often as you want on a bit o' yellow hair, but it still comes blood the next time so why bother, *he'd* say. And *I'd* say it too. Here. (*He kisses her again and lets her go.*) There you are, girly: I've given you all you should get from a soldier. Say 'Thank you, boy', and that's that.

ANNIE (*still hard*). Thank you boy . . . You know it, don't you? All I should get. All I ever have got. Why should I want more? You stand up honest, you do, and it's a good thing too, 'cos you're old enough.

ATTERCLIFFE (*with a wry smile*). H'm. I am and all. Good night.

He starts making up his bed and undressing. SPARKY *has sat up and is listening. As* ANNIE *is standing still,* ATTERCLIFFE *starts talking to her again.*

ATTERCLIFFE. Girly. When I was a young lad I got married to a wife. And she slept with a greengrocer. He was the best looker (like *he's* the best looker) – (*he points towards* HURST'S *box*) – or any road that's what *she* said. *I* saw him four foot ten inch tall and he looked like a rat grinning through a brush; but he sold good green apples and he fed the people and he fed my wife. I didn't do neither. So now I'm a dirty old bastard in a red coat and blue breeches and that's all about it. Blood, y'see: killing. Good night.

He has now undressed and lies down to sleep immediately.
ANNIE *stands for a minute, then subsides to a crouching position, in tears.*
SPARKY *creeps out of his box.*

SPARKY. Tst tst tst, Annie. Stop crying: come here.

ANNIE. Don't talk to me, go to bed, I can't bear wi' no more of you.

SPARKY. Annie, Annie, look now, I want to talk. I'm not deaf, y'know, and I'm not that drunk, I mean I've been drunker, I mean I can stand, ha ha, one foot and all, I'm a stork, look at me – (*He tries to balance on one foot*). Him at the far end – don't you worry for *him*, Annie – why, he's not mortal any more, he's like God, ent he? And God – (*He looks towards* MUSGRAVE'S *light*) – hello, God's asleep.

ANNIE. God?

SPARKY. He's put his light out. Look,

ANNIE. That's where the serjeant is.

SPARKY. That's right. I never thought he'd sleep. *I* can't sleep . . . what have you got against me?

ANNIE (*surprised*). Nowt that I know.

SPARKY. But you didn't come to me, did you? I mean, you asked *him* and he said no, I asked *you* and you said no. That's all wrong. I mean, you know what the Black Musgrave'd call that, don't you – *he'd* say anarchy!

ANNIE. *He'd say*? He?

MUSGRAVE *groans in his bed.*

Every one of you swaggering lobsters, that serjeant squats in your gobs like an old wife stuck in a fireplace. What's the matter with you all!

SPARKY. Ssh ssh, keep it quiet. Come down here . . .

He leads her as far as possible from the other two.

Listen.

ANNIE. What for?

SPARKY. Snoring. Him? Him? Good, two snorings. They're asleep . . . I told you in the bar, y'know, they call me Sparky – name and nature – Sparky has his laugh. . . . A man can laugh, because or else he might well howl – and howling's not for men but for dogs, wolves, seagulls – like o' that, ent it?

ANNIE. You mean that you're frightened?

SPARKY (*with a sort of nervous self-realisation*). Aye, begod, d'you know: I am. God's not here, he's put his light out: so I can tell you, love: I *am.* Hey, not of the war, bullets in the far Empire, that's not the reason, don't think it. They even give me a medal, silver, to prove so. But I'll tell you, I'm – here, kiss me, will you, quickly, I oughtn't to be talking . . . I think I've gone daft.

ANNIE (*who is looking at him curiously but fascinated*). All right, I will . . .

She kisses him, and he holds her.

MUSGRAVE (*in clear categorical tones, though in his sleep*). Twenty-five men. Nine women. Twenty-five men. No children. No.

ANNIE (*in a sudden uprush*). Look, boy, there was a time *I* had a soldier, he made jokes, he sang songs and all – ah, *he* lived yes-sarnt no-sarnt three-bags-full-serjeant, but he called it one damned joke. God damn you, he was killed! Aye, and in your desert Empire – so what did *that* make?

SPARKY. I don't know . . .

ANNIE. It made a twisted little thing dead that nobody laughed at. A little withered clover – three in one it made. There was me, and there was him: and a baby in the ground. Bad shape. Dead.

She can say nothing more and he comforts her silently a moment.

SPARKY (*his mind working*). Why, Annie . . . Annie . . . you as well: another one not paid for . . . O, I wish *I* could pay. Say, suppose I paid for yours; why, maybe you could pay for mine.

ANNIE. I don't understand.

SPARKY (*following his thought in great disturbance of mind*). It *wouldn't* be anarchy, you know; he can't be right there! All it would be, is: *you* live and *I* live – we don't need his duty, we don't need his Word – a dead man's a dead man! We could call it *all* paid for! Your life and my life – make our *own* road, we don't follow nobody.

ANNIE. What are you talking about?

SPARKY (*relapsing into his despair again*). Oh God, I don't know. God's gone to sleep, but when he wakes up again –

ANNIE (*bewildered but compassionate*). Oh quiet, boy, be quiet, easy, easy.

She stoops over him, where he has crumpled into a corner, and they embrace again with passion.

MUSGRAVE (*now shouting in his sleep*). Fire, fire! Fire, fire, London's burning, London's burning!

MRS. HITCHCOCK, *in a nightdress and robe, and carrying a tumbler, hurries into his bedroom.*

MRS. HITCHCOCK. What's the matter?

She lights his candle.

MUSGRAVE (*sitting up and talking very clearly as if it made sense*). Burning. Burning. One minute from now, and you carry out your orders – get *that* one! *Get* her! Who says she's a child! We've got her in the book, she's old enough to kill! You will carry out your orders. Thirty seconds. Count the time. (*He is looking at his watch.*) Twenty-six . . . twenty-three . . .

MRS. HITCHCOCK (*very alarmed*). Serjeant – Serjeant –

MUSGRAVE. Be quiet. Twenty . . . Eighteen . . . I'm on duty, woman. I'm timing the end of the world. Ten more seconds, sir . . . Five . . . three . . . two . . . one.

He lets out a great cry of agony and falls back on the bed. All in the stable hear and take notice. ATTERCLIFFE *turns over again to sleep.* HURST *sits up in alarm.* ANNIE *and* SPARKY *stand apart from each other in surprise.*

ANNIE. Sparky, it's your God. He's hurt.

SPARKY *sits staring and gasping, till* ANNIE *pulls him to her again.*

MRS. HITCHCOCK. What are you playing at – you'll wake up the town!

MUSGRAVE *shivers and moans.*

MRS. HITCHCOCK (*shaking him gently*). Come on – it's a nightmare. Wake up and let's get rid of it. Come on, come on.

MUSGRAVE. Leave me alone. I wasn't asleep.

MRS. HITCHCOCK. You warn't awake, any road.

MUSGRAVE. Mind your own business.

MRS. HITCHCOCK. I thought you might be poorly.

MUSGRAVE. No . . . No . . . (*Suddenly*) But it *will* come, won't it?

MRS. HITCHCOCK. What will?

MUSGRAVE. The end of the world? You'll tell me it's not material, but if you could come to it, in control; I mean, numbers and order, like so many ranks this side, so many that, properly dressed, steadiness on parade, so that whether you knew you was right, or you knew you was wrong – you'd know it, and you'd stand. (*He shivers.*) Get me summat to eat.

MRS. HITCHCOCK. I got you a hot grog. Here. (*She gives him a tumbler.*)

MUSGRAVE. What – what . . .?

MRS. HITCHCOCK. I take it at nights for me bad back. I heard you calling so I brought it in. Have a biscuit.

She gives him a biscuit from her dressing gown pocket.

MUSGRAVE. Aye, I will . . . (*He eats and drinks.*) That's better . . . You *do* understand me, don't you? Look, if you're the right-marker to the Company and you're marching to the right, you can't see the others, so you follow the orders you can hear and hope you hear them true. When I was a recruit

I found myself once half across the square alone – *they'd* marched the other way and I'd never heard the word!

MRS. HITCHCOCK. You ought to lie down. You *are* poorly, I can tell. Easy, Serjeant, easy.

MUSGRAVE (*relaxing again*). Easy . . . easy . . .

She draws the blanket over him and sits soothing him to sleep.

SPARKY (*with a sudden access of resolution*). Annie, I don't care. Let him wake when he wants to. All I'll do this time is to stand and *really* laugh. Listen to this one, because here's what I'll be laughing at. There was these four lads, y'see, and they made it out they'd have a strong night all night in the town, each boozer in turn, pay-day. And the first one in the first boozer, he says: 'Each man drinks my choice,' he says. 'One sup of arsenic to every man's glass' – and *that's* what they've to drink. Well, one of them, he drinks and he dies, next man drinks and *he* dies, what about the third? Has he to drink to that rule? 'Cos they'd *made* it a rule – each man to the first man's choice.

HURST *has left his box and crept up and is now listening to this.*

ANNIE. I don't know –

SPARKY. Neither do I. But I can tell you what *I'd* do.

ANNIE. What?

SPARKY (*with a switch to hard seriousness*). I'd get out of it, quick. Aye, and with you. Look, love, its snowing, we can't leave the town now. But you could bed me down somewheres, I mean, like, hide; bide *with* me while it's all over, and then get me some clothes and we'd go – I mean, like, go to London? What about London? You've never been to London?

ANNIE. Bide hid while *what's* all over? What's going to happen?

SPARKY. Eh, that's the question. I wish I could tell you. It's Black Jack's work, not mine.

ANNIE. Bad work, likely?

SPARKY. Likely . . . I don't know. D'you know, I never *asked!* You see, he's like God, and it's as if *we* were like angels – *angels*, ha, ha! But that's no joke no more for me. This is funnier nor *I* can laugh at, Annie, and if I bide longer here, I'm *really* wild-wood mad. So get me out of it, quick!

ANNIE (*decisively*). I will. I'm frightened. Pull your clothes on, Sparky. I'll hide you.

SPARKY. Good love, good –

ANNIE. But you'll not leave me behind?

He has started dressing, very confusedly, putting his tunic on first.

SPARKY. No.

ANNIE. Swear it.

He has his trousers ready to step into. He lets them fall while he takes her for a moment in his arms:

SPARKY. Sworn.

HURST *nips in and seizes the trousers.*

(*Releasing* ANNIE) Now then, sharp. Hey, where's me trousers?

HURST. Here!

SPARKY. What's the goddamn – give 'em back, you dirty –

HURST (*triumphantly*). Come and get 'em, Sparky! Heh, you'll be the grand deserter, won't you, running bare-arsed over the moor in six-foot drifts of snow!

SPARKY. Give me them!

He grabs one end of the trousers and a farcical tug-o'-war begins.

HURST (*in high malice*). A man and a soldier! Jump, natter, twitch, like a clockwork puppet for three parts of the night.

but the last night of all, you *run*! You little closhy coward.

ATTERCLIFFE *has woken and tries to intervene.*

ATTERCLIFFE. What the hell's the row – easy, easy, *hold* it!
SPARKY. He's got my bloody trousers!

He gives a great tug on the trousers and pulls them away, HURST *falling down.*

HURST. I'm going to *do* you, Sparky.

His hand falls on SPARKY'S *belt, with bayonet scabbard attached, which is lying on the floor. He gets up, drawing the bayonet.*

ANNIE. No, no, stop him!
ATTERCLIFFE. Drop that bayonet!

ANNIE *mixes in, seizing* HURST'S *wrist and biting it. The bayonet drops to the floor.* ATTERCLIFFE *snatches it and* HURST *jumps upon him. Together they fall against* SPARKY *and all three crash to the floor.* SPARKY *gives a terrifying, choking cry.*
MUSGRAVE *leaps up in the bedroom. Those on the forestage all draw back, appalled, from* SPARKY'S *dead body.*

MUSGRAVE (*to* MRS. HITCHCOCK). Stay where you are.

He leaves the bedroom.

HURST. He's dead. He's dead. *I* didn't do it. Not me. No.
ATTERCLIFFE. Dead?
HURST. Of course he's dead. He's stuck in the gut. That's you. Your hand. You killed him.
ATTERCLIFFE. I can't have.
HURST. You did.
ATTERCLIFFE (*stupidly*). I've got the bayonet.
HURST. Aye, and you've killed him.
ATTERCLIFFE. O Holy God!

MUSGRAVE *enters from the house.* MRS. HITCHCOCK *has left the bedroom.*

MUSGRAVE. What going on?

HURST. Sparky's been killed.

MUSGRAVE. *What!* How?

HURST. His own bayonet. He was deserting. I tried to stop him. Then *he* –

He points to ATTERCLIFFE.

MUSGRAVE (*to* ATTERCLIFFE). Well?

ATTERCLIFFE (*hopelessly*). Here's the bayonet. I got holding it, Serjeant. I did. It's always me. You can call it an accident. But *I* know what that means, it means that it –

MUSGRAVE. Shut up. You said deserting?

HURST *nods.*

What's *she* doing here? Was she with him?

HURST *nods.*

Aye, aye . . . Desertion. Fornication. It's not material. He's dead. Hide him away.

HURST. Where?

MUSGRAVE. In the midden at back of the yard. And don't show no lights while you're doing it. Hurry.

HURST (*to* ATTERCLIFFE). Come on.

ATTERCLIFFE. Holy God, Holy God!

They carry the body out.

MUSGRAVE (*to* ANNIE, *unpleasantly*). Oh, you can shake, you can quiver, you can open your mouth like a quicksand and all – blubbering and trouble – but *I've* got to think, and *I've* got to do.

MRS. HITCHCOCK *enters from the house. She is carrying* MUSGRAVE'S *tunic, hat, and boots, which she puts down.*

Missus, come here. There's things going wrong, but don't ask me what. Will you trust me?

She looks at him searchingly and gives a short nod.

Get hold of this lassie, take her upstairs, lock her in a cupboard, and keep quiet about it. I've got a right reason: you'll know it in good time. Do as I tell you and you won't take no harm.

MRS. HITCHCOCK. The end of the world, already.

MUSGRAVE. What's that? D'ye hear what I say?

MRS. HITCHCOCK. Oh aye, I heard you.

She takes the shuddering ANNIE *by the hand, and then looks sharply at her fingers.*

Hey-ey-ey, this here, it's blood.

MUSGRAVE. I know. I repeat it: don't ask me.

ANNIE *looks at* MUSGRAVE *and at* MRS. HITCHCOCK, *then licks her hand, laughing in a childish fashion.*

MRS. HITCHCOCK. Come away in, Annie . . . Aye, I'll go and lock her up . . . It might be the best thing. I've got to trust you, haven't I? I've always praised religion.

She takes ANNIE *away, into the house.* MUSGRAVE *sits down suddenly, with his head in his hands. The* BARGEE *creeps in from the yard and sits beside him, in a similar attitude.*

BARGEE (*singing softly*).

Here we set like birds in the wilderness,
birds in the –

MUSGRAVE *sits up, looks at him, realises who it is, and grabs him by the throat.*

BARGEE (*struggling free*). It's all right, bully, it's only Old Joe.

MUSGRAVE (*relaxing, but still menacing*). Oh it is, is it? Well?

BARGEE (*significantly*). I was thinking, like, if I wor you, *I* wouldn't just set down in a stable, not now I wouldn't, no.

MUSGRAVE. Why not?

BARGEE. *I* see your jolly muckers, over there, mucking in the muck-pile, eh? But if they turned theirselves around and looked at the coach-house –

MUSGRAVE *leaps up in alarm.*

MUSGRAVE. What about the coach-house?

BARGEE. There's bars at its windows : and there's a crowbar at the bars – listen!

A crash of glass offstage from the yard.

That's the glass gone now! If you're quick, you can catch 'em!

MUSGRAVE *has run to the yard side of the stage.*

MUSGRAVE (*calling to offstage*). Get to the coach-house, get round the back! Quick! Quick!

He runs off in great excitement.
More crashes of glass, shouting and banging.
The BARGEE *watches what is happening in the yard, leaping up and down in high delight.*

BARGEE. Go on, catch 'em, two to the back and the serjeant to the door, open the padlock, swing back the wicket – one little laddie, he's trapped in the window – head in, feet out – pull him down, Serjeant, pull him down, soldiers – boot up, fist down, tie him in a bundle – oh me pretty roses, oh me blood-red flowers o' beauty!

The two SOLDIERS *hurry back, with* WALSH *frogmarched between them, his hands bunched up and tied behind his back.* MUSGRAVE *follows. All are panting. They throw* WALSH *down.*

MUSGRAVE. What about the others?

HURST. Run away, Serjeant.

ATTERCLIFFE. Nigh on a dozen of 'em.

HURST. Ran down the alley.

MUSGRAVE. Let's have a look at this one! Oho, so it's *you!* What were you after?

WALSH (*grinning*). What d'you think, lobster?

MUSGRAVE. Our little Gatling? Isn't that right?

WALSH. That's right, boy, you're sharp.

MUSGRAVE (*quieter*). But *you're* not sharp, brother, and I'm going to tell you why.

Shouting and shrill whistles, off.

HURST. It's that Constable's out, and his Specials and all – listen! Hey, we'd better get dressed.

He starts huddling on his tunic and trousers.

MUSGRAVE (*to* WALSH). Chasing your friends. He'll be coming here, shortly.

Whistles again.

CONSTABLE (*offstage, in the house*). Open up, Mrs. Hitchcock, open up – name of the Law!

MUSGRAVE. Ah, here he is. Now he asked me this evening to kidnap you for the Army. But *I* told you we was brothers, didn't I? So watch while I prove it. (*To* HURST.) Take him out and hide him.

HURST (*taken aback*). Him in the midden too?

MUSGRAVE. Don't be a fool. Do as you're told.

WALSH. Wait – wait a minute.

MUSGRAVE (*furiously*). Go with him, you damned nignog. Would ye rather trust the Constable?

WALSH (*very puzzled*). What are you on, for God's sake?

MUSGRAVE. Don't waste time! (*He pushes* WALSH *and barks*

at HURST.) Get him in that woodshed. God, what a shower o' tortoises!

HURST *hustles* WALSH *out to the yard.* MUSGRAVE *turns on* ATTERCLIFFE.

You get your trousers on.

ATTERCLIFFE *obeys.* MRS. HITCHCOCK *comes in, very agitated.*

MRS. HITCHCOCK. The Constable's here, he's running through the house.

MUSGRAVE. Then send him to me! It's in control, in control, woman. I *know* all about it!

MRS. HITCHCOCK *goes back into the house.*

ATTERCLIFFE. Musgrave, what are you doing?

MUSGRAVE. I'm doing what comes next and that's all I've got time for.

ATTERCLIFFE (*in a gush of despair*). But he was killed, you see, killed. Musgrave, don't you see, that wipes the whole thing out, wiped out, washed out, finished.

MUSGRAVE. *No!*

MRS. HITCHCOCK *and the* CONSTABLE *hurry in from the house.*

CONSTABLE. Ah, Serjeant, what's happened? Saw a gang breaking in at the back of this coach-house. What's kept in the coach-house? (*To* MRS. HITCHCOCK.)

MRS. HITCHCOCK. The Serjeant's got his –

MUSGRAVE. I've got my gear.

MRS. HITCHCOCK. Hello, here's the Parson.

The PARSON *hurries in from the house.*

PARSON. Constable, what's going on?

CONSTABLE. I think it's beginning, sir. I think it's the riots.

PARSON. At this hour of the morning?

CONSTABLE. I've sent word to the Mayor.

He starts making a rapid report to the PARSON. *The* BARGEE *sidles up to* MUSGRAVE.

BARGEE. Don't forget Old Joe. I brought the warning. Let me in on a share of it, go on, there's a bully.

MUSGRAVE. Get out, or you'll get hurt!

The MAYOR *hurries in from the house.*

MAYOR. This is bad, it's bloody bad. How did it start? Never mind that now. What steps have you taken?

CONSTABLE. Me Deputy-Specials all around the streets, but I've not got enough of 'em and they're frightened – that's frank. I *warned* you, Your Worship.

MAYOR. Question is this: can you hold the town safe while twelve o'clock mid-day?

CONSTABLE. Nay I don't know.

MAYOR. The telegraph's working.

MUSGRAVE. The telegraph!

MAYOR. Aye, there's a thaw begun. Thank God for that: they've mended the broken wire on top of the moor. So I sent word for the Dragoons. They'll come as fast as they can, but not afore twelve I shouldn't think, so we've *got* to hold this town!

MUSGRAVE. Six hours, thereabouts. Keep 'em quiet now, they may bide. Mr. Mayor, I'll do it for you.

MAYOR. How?

MUSGRAVE. I'll do what I'm paid for : start a recruiting-meeting. Look, we had 'em last night as merry as Christmas in here, why not this morning? Flags, drums, shillings, sovereigns – hey, start the drum! Top o' the market-place, make a jolly speech to 'em!

MAYOR. Me?

HURST *begins beating the drum outside in the yard.*

MUSGRAVE. You! You, Parson, too. Mrs. Hitchcock, free beer to the crowd!

PARSON. No!

MAYOR (*catching the idea*). *Aye*, missus, bring it! *I'll* pay for it and all!

MUSGRAVE (*to the* BARGEE). *You*, if you want to help, you can carry a flag. (*To* ATTERCLIFFE.) Get him a flag!

Exit ATTERCLIFFE. *Enter* HURST, *drumming furiously*.

We'll *all* carry flags. Fetch me me tunic.

MRS. HITCHCOCK. Here it is, I brought it.

MUSGRAVE (*quite wild with excitement*). Flags, ribbons, bunches o' ribbons, glamourise 'em, glory!

ATTERCLIFFE *hurries in from the yard, with his arms full of colours. He hands these out all round.*

BARGEE. Rosebuds of Old England!

MAYOR. Loyal hearts and true!

PARSON. The Lord mighty in battle!

MUSGRAVE. GOD SAVE THE QUEEN!

General noise, bustle and confusion.

Act Three

SCENE ONE

The market-place.

Early morning. In the centre of the stage is a practicable feature – the centre-piece of the market-place. It is a sort of Victorian clock-tower-cum-lamppost-cum-market-cross, and stands on a raised plinth. There is a ladder leaning against it. On the plinth are the soldiers' boxes and a coil of rope. The front of the plinth is draped with bunting, and other colours are leaning against the centre-piece in an impressive disposition.
When the scene opens, the stage is filled with noise and movement HURST *is beating his drum, the* MAYOR, *the* PARSON *and* MUSGRAVE *are mounting the plinth, and* ATTERCLIFFE *is up already, making the last arrangements. The* CONSTABLE *takes up his stand beside the centre-piece, as does* HURST. *The* BARGEE *is hopping about on the forestage.*
The SOLDIERS *are all now properly dressed, the* MAYOR *has put on his cocked hat and red robe and chain, and the* PARSON *his gown and bands, and carries a Bible. They are all wearing bright cockades.*
The role of the BARGEE *in this scene is important. As there is no crowd, the speeches are delivered straight out to the audience, and the* BARGEE *acts as a kind of fugleman to create the crowd-reactions. Noises-off indicated in the dialogue are rather unrealistic – as it were, token-noises only.*
At one side of the stage there is an upper-storey window.

BARGEE (*casting his cap*).

Hip hip hooroar
Hark hark the drums do bark
The Hungry Army's coming to town
Lead 'em in with a Holy Book
A golden chain and a scarlet gown.

Here they are on a winter's morning, you've got six kids at home crying out for bread, you've got a sour cold wife and no fire and no breakfast: and you're too damn miserable even to fight – if there's owt else at all to take your mind off it – so here you are, you lucky people, in your own old market-place, a real live lovely circus, with real live golden sovereigns in somebody's pocket and real live taddy ale to be doled out to the bunch of you!

MRS. HITCHCOCK *enters, trundling a beer-barrel.*

Oh, it's for free, you can be certain o' that, there's no strings to this packet – let's lend you a hand wi' that, missus!

He helps her roll the barrel to one side of the centre-piece, where she chocks it level and sits down on it. She also has a hand-basket full of tankards. The BARGEE *comes back downstage.*

There we are, then. And here *you* are, the streets is filling, roll up, roll up, and wallow in the lot! I'll tell you the word when to cheer.

The platform party is now all in place. The drum gives a final roll. The MAYOR *steps forward.*

CONSTABLE. Silence for the Mayor!

BARGEE. Long live His Worship, who gives us food and clothing and never spares to meet the people with a smile! Hooroar!

Three boos, off.

Boo, boo, boo? Don't be so previous, now; he'll surprise us

all yet, boys. Benevolence and responsibility. Silence for the Mayor!

MAYOR. All right. Now then. It's been a hard winter. I know there's a bit of a thaw this morning, but it's not over yet, there may be worse to come. Although you might not think it, I'm as keen and eager as any o' you to get the pits working again, so we can all settle down in peace to a good roast and baked 'taters and a good pudding and the rest of it. But I'm not here to talk strikes today.

A noise off.

BARGEE (*interpreting*). He says: 'Who says strikes, it's a bloody lockout.'

CONSTABLE. Silence for the Mayor!

BARGEE. Silence for His Worship!

MAYOR. I said I'm not up here to talk on that today. Serjeant Musgrave, on my right, has come to town to find men for the Queen. Now that's a good opportunity – it's a *grand* opportunity. It's up to you to take it. By God, if I was a young lad in a town without work, you'd not catch me thinking twice –

BARGEE. He says: 'There's only one man drives the work away in this town.'

The CONSTABLE *steps forward, but the* BARGEE *forestalls him.*

Silence for the Mayor!

MAYOR. All right. You think I'm playing it crooked all the time – *I* know.

A cheer off.

But listen to this: (*He holds up a jingling money-bag.*) Here's real gold. It rings true to me, it rings true to you, and there's one o' these for every lad as volunteers. That's straight. It's from the shoulder. It pulls no punches. Take it or throw it away – I'm set up here and waiting. (Parson, tell 'em *your* piece now.) And keep quiet while the Rector's at you: he talks good sense and you need it. If you can't give *me* credit, at least you can give *him* some, for considering what's best for the community. Go on, Parson: tell 'em.

He retires and the PARSON *steps forward.*

PARSON. 'And Jesus said, I come not to bring peace but a sword.' I know very well that the times are difficult. As your minister of religion, and as a magistrate, it is my business to be aware of these matters. But we must remember that this town is only one very small locality in our great country.

BARGEE. Very true, very true.

Two cheers, off.

PARSON. And if our country is great, and I for one am sure that it *is* great, it is great because of the greatness of its responsibilities. They are world wide. They are noble. They are the responsibilities of a first-class power.

BARGEE. Keep 'em there, Reverend! First-class for ever! Give a cheer, you boys!

Three cheers, very perfunctory.

And the crowd roars! Every hat in the air, you've struck 'em in the running nerve, hooroar!

PARSON. Therefore, I say, therefore: when called to shoulder our country's burdens we should do it with a glancing eye and a leaping heart, to draw the sword with gladness, thinking nothing of our petty differences and grievances – but all united under one brave flag, going forth in Christian resolution, and showing a manly spirit! The Empire calls! Greatness is at hand! Serjeant Musgrave will take down the names of any men willing, if you'll file on to the platform in an orderly fashion, in the name of the Father, the Son and mumble mumble mumble . . .

He retires. There is a pause.

MUSGRAVE. Perhaps, Mr. Mayor, before we start enrolling names, it might be as well if I was to say a few words first, like, outlining the type of service the lads is likely to find, overseas, and so forth?

The SLOW COLLIER *slouches in, and up to the base of the plinth.*

SLOW COLLIER. Have you got my name down?

MUSGRAVE. No. Not yet.

SLOW COLLIER. Are you sure of that ?

MUSGRAVE. Aye, I'm sure. D'you want me to take it?

SLOW COLLIER. Some of us was a bit full, like, last night in the boozer.

MUSGRAVE. A man's pleasuring, friend, that's all. No harm in that?

SLOW COLLIER (*thrusting forward his hat with the cockade in it*). Then what's this? Eh? Someone gave me this.

MUSGRAVE (*laughs*). Oh I'll tell you what that means: you drank along of me – that's all that it means – and you promised you'd come and hear me this morning. Well, here you are.

SLOW COLLIER. Ah. Provisional. Aye. I thought that's what it was. Provisional.

The PUGNACIOUS COLLIER *slouchse in.*

PUGNACIOUS COLLIER. Provisional or not, we're not signing nowt without we've heard more. So go on then, soldier, tell us. Prove it's better to be shot nor starve, *we'll* listen to you, man, 'cos we're ready to believe. And more of us and all.

CRIES OFF. Aye. Aye. Aye. Tell us.

BARGEE. Go on, Serjeant, tell us. It's a long strong tale, quiet while he tells it – quiet!

MUSGRAVE. Now there's more tales than one about the Army,

and a lot of funny jokers to run around and spread 'em, too. Aye, aye, we've all heard of 'em, we know all about 'em, and it's not my job this morning to swear to you what's true and what's not true. O' *course* you'll find there's an RSM here or a Provost-sarnt there what makes you cut the grass wi' nail-scissors, or dust the parade-ground with a toothbrush. It's all the bull, it's all in the game – but it's not what sends me here and it's not what put *these* on my arm, and it's nowt at all to do with *my* life, or these two with me, or any o' yours. So easy, me boys, don't think it. (*To the* COLLIERS.) There was another lad wi' *you*, in and out last night. He ought to be here. (*To the* BARGEE.) Go and fetch him, will you? You know where he is.

BARGEE (*finger to nose*). Ah. Ha ha. Aye aye.

He slips out conspiratorily.

MUSGRAVE (*continues his speech*). I said, easy me boys, and don't think it. Because there's *work* in the Army, and bull's not right work, you can believe me on that – it's just foolery – any smart squaddy can carry it away like a tuppenny-ha'penny jam jar. So I'll tell you what the *work* is – open it up!

ATTERCLIFFE *flings open one of the boxes. It is packed with rifles. He takes one out and tosses it to* MUSGRAVE.

MUSGRAVE. Now this is the rifle. This is what we term the butt of the rifle. This is the barrel. This here's the magazine. And this – (*he indicates the trigger*) – you should know what *this is*, you should know what it does . . . Well, the rifle's a good weapon, it's new, quick, accurate. This is the bayonet – (*he fixes his bayonet*) – it kills men smart, it's good and it's beautiful. But I've more to show than a rifle. Open it up!

ATTERCLIFFE *opens a second case. It contains a Gatling gun and tripod mounting.*

This is the newest, this is the smartest, call it the most beautiful. It's a Gatling gun, this. Watch how it works!

ATTERCLIFFE *secures the gun to its mounting.*

ATTERCLIFFE. The rounds are fed to the chambers, which are arranged in a radial fashion, by means of a hopper-shaped aperture, *here*. Now pay attention while I go through the preliminary process of loading.

He goes through the preliminary process of loading.

MUSGRAVE (*his urgency increasing all the time*). The point being that here we've got a gun that doesn't shoot like: *Bang*, rattle-click-up-the-spout-what're-we-waiting-for, *bang!* But: Bang-bang-bang-bang-bang-bang-bang-bang-*bang* – and there's not a man alive in the whole of this market-place. Modern times. Progress. Three hundred and fifty rounds in one minute – *flat!*

The BARGEE *re-enters, soft-footed.*

MUSGRAVE (*quickly to him*). Is he coming?

The BARGEE *nods, finger to lips.*

ATTERCLIFFE. Now then, you see, the gun's loaded.
MUSGRAVE. It didn't take long, you see.
ATTERCLIFFE. No.

HURST *gives a roll on the drums.*
ATTERCLIFFE *swivels the gun to face out into the audience.*
MUSGRAVE *loads his rifle with a clip of cartridges.*

MUSGRAVE (*his voice very taut and hard*). The question remains as to the *use* of these weapons! (*He pushes his rifle-bolt home.*) You'll ask me: what's their purpose? Seeing we've beat the Russians in the Crimea, there's no war with France (there *may* be, but there isn't yet), and Germany's our friend, who do we have to fight? *Well*, the Reverend answered *that* for you, in his good short words. Me and my three lads – two lads, I'd say rather – we belong to a regiment is a few thousand miles from here, in a little country without much importance except from the point of view that there's a Union Jack flies over it and the people of that country can write British Subject after their names. And that makes us proud!

ATTERCLIFFE. I tell you it makes us proud!

HURST. We live in tattered tents in the rain, we eat rotten food, there's knives in the dark streets and blood on the floors of the hospitals, but we stand tall and proud: because of why we are there.

ATTERCLIFFE. Because we're there to serve our duty.

MUSGRAVE. A soldier's duty is a soldier's life.

WALSH *enters at the extreme rear of the stage and walks slowly up behind the others and listens.*
A roll on the drum.

MUSGRAVE. A soldier's life is to lay it down, against the enemies of his Queen,

A roll on the drum.

against the invaders of his home,

A roll on the drum.

against slavery, cruelty, tyrants.

A roll on the drum.

HURST. You put on the uniform and you give your life away, and who do you give it to?

ATTERCLIFFE. You give it to your duty.

MUSGRAVE. And you give it to your people, for peace, and for honesty.

A roll on the arum.

MUSGRAVE. That's *my* book. (*He turns on the* MAYOR.) What's *yours?*

MAYOR (*very taken aback*). Eh? What? I'm not a reading man, but it *sounds* all right . . . strong. Strong . . .

MUSGRAVE (*to the* PARSON). What about *yours?*

PARSON (*dubiously*). You speak with enthusiasm, yes. I hope you'll be listened to.

MUSGRAVE (*at the top of his passion*). By God, I hope I am! D'ye hear me, d'ye hear me, d'ye hear me – I'm the Queen of England's man, and I'm wearing her coat and I know her Book backwards. I'm Black Jack Musgrave, me, the hardest serjeant of the line – I work my life to bugle and drum, for eighteen years I fought for one flag only, salute it in the morning, can you haul it down at dark? The Last Post of a living life? Look – I'll show it to you all. And I'll *dance* for you beneath it – hoist up the flag, boy – up, up, *up!*

ATTERCLIFFE *has nipped up the ladder, holding the rope. He loops the rope over the cross-bar of the lamp-bracket, drops to the plinth again, flings open the lid of the big box, and hauls on the rope.*

HURST *beats frantically on his drum. The rope is attached to the contents of the box, and these are jerked up to the cross-bar and reveal themselves as an articulated skeleton dressed in a soldier's tunic and trousers, the rope noosed round the neck. The* PEOPLE *draw back in horror.* MUSGRAVE *begins to dance, waving his rifle, his face contorted with demoniac fury.*

MUSGRAVE (*as he dances, sings, with mounting emphasis*).

Up he goes and no one knows
How to bring him downwards
Dead man's feet
Over the street
Riding the roofs
And crying down your chimneys

Up he goes and no one knows
Who it was that rose him
But white and red
He waves his head
He sits on your back
And you'll never never lose him
Up he goes and no one knows
How to bring him downwards.

He breaks off at the climax of the song, and stands panting. The drum stops.

That'll do. That'll do for *that*. (*He beckons gently to the* PEOPLE.) You can come back. Come back. Come back. We're all quiet now. But nobody move out of this market-place. You saw the gun loaded. Well, it's on a very quick swivel and the man behind it's well trained. (*He gestures with his rifle towards the platform party.*) And *I've* won a regimental cup four year running for small-arms marksmanship. So be good, and be gentle, *all* of you.

That checks the BARGEE, *who made a move. The* MAYOR *seems to be about to speak.*

Right, Mr. Mayor – I'll explain the whole business.

PARSON (*in a smaller voice than usual*). Business? What business, sir? Do you intend to imply you are *threatening* us with these weapons?

MAYOR. The man's gone balmy. Constable, do summat, grab him, quick!

The CONSTABLE *makes an indecisive move.*

MUSGRAVE. Be *quiet*. I shan't warn agen. (*To the* MAYOR *and the* PARSON.) You two. Get down there! Constable, *there!*

He gestures peremptorily and the three of them obey him, moving downstage to stand facing the platform and covered by the gun.

Now I said I'll explain. So listen. (*He points to the skeleton.*) This, up here, was a comrade of mine – of ours. At least, he was till a few months since. He was killed, being there for his duty, in the country I was telling you about, where the regiment is stationed. It's not right a colony, you know, it's a sort of Protectorate, but British, y'know, British. This, up here, he was walking down a street latish at night, he'd been to the opera – *you've* got a choral society in this town, I daresay – well, he was only a soldier, but North Country, he was full of music, so he goes to the opera. And on his way again to camp he was shot in the back. And it's not surprising, neither: there was patriots abroad, anti-British, subversive; like they didn't dare to shoot him to his face. He was daft to be out alone, wasn't he? Out of bounds, after curfew.

ATTERCLIFFE (*with suppressed frenzy*). Get on to the words as matter, serjeant!

MUSGRAVE (*turning on him fiercely*). *I'm* talking now; you wait your turn! . . . So we *come* to the words as matter. He was the third to be shot that week. He was the fifteenth that month. In the back and all. Add to which he was young, he was liked, he sang songs, they say, and he joked and he laughed – he was a good soldier, too, else *I'd* not have bothered (we'll leave out his sliding off to the opera WOL, but by and large good, and I've got standards). So at twelve o'clock at night they beat up the drums and sounded the calls and called out the guard and the guard calls us *all* out, and the road is red and slippery, and every soldier in the camp no longer in the camp but in the streets of that city, rifle-butts, bayonets, every street cut off for eight blocks north and west the opera-house. And that's how it began.

HURST (*the frenzy rising*). The streets is empty, but the houses is full. He says, 'no undue measures, minimum violence', he says. 'But bring in the killers.'

ATTERCLIFFE. The killers are gone, they've gone miles off in that time – *sporting* away, right up in the mountains, I told you at the time.

MUSGRAVE. That's not material, there's one man is dead, but there's *everyone's* responsible.

HURST. So bring the *lot* in! It's easy, they're all in bed, kick the front doors down, knock 'em on the head, boys, chuck 'em in the wagons.

ATTERCLIFFE. I didn't know she was only a little kid, there was scores of 'em on that staircase, pitch-dark, trampling, screaming, they're all of 'em screaming, what are we to do?

HURST. Knock 'em on the head, boy, chuck 'em in the wagons.

ATTERCLIFFE. How was I to tell she was only a little kid?

MUSGRAVE (*bringing it to an end*). THAT'S NOT MATERIAL! You were told to bring 'em in. If you killed her, you killed her! She was just one, and who cares a damn for that! Stay in your place and keep your hands on that Gatling. We've got to have order here, whatever there was *there;* and I can tell you it wasn't order . . . (*To* HURST.) You, take a rifle. Leave your drum down.

HURST *jumps on the plinth, takes a rifle and loads.*

We've *got* to have order. So I'll just tell you quietly how many there were was put down as injured – that's badly hurt, hospital, we don't count knocks and bruises, any o' that. Twenty-five men. Nine women. *No* children, whatever *he* says. She was a fully grown girl, and she had a known record as an associate of terrorists. That was her. Then four men, one of them elderly, turned out to have died too. Making five. Not so very many. Dark streets. Natural surge of rage.

HURST. We didn't find the killers.

MUSGRAVE. Of course we didn't find 'em. Not *then* we didn't, any road. We didn't even know 'em. But *I* know 'em, now.

(*He turns on* WALSH.) So what's *your* opinion?

MAYOR. He's not balmy, he's mad, he's stark off his nut.

PARSON. Why doesn't somebody do something, Constable?

Noises off.

MUSGRAVE (*indicates* WALSH). I'm talking to *him*.

CONSTABLE (*very shakily*). I shall have to ask you to – to come down off this platform, Sarnt Musgrave. It looks to me like your – your meeting's got out of hand.

HURST (*covering the* CONSTABLE). Aye, it has.

MUSGRAVE (*to* WALSH). Go on, brother. Tell us.

WALSH *climbs up at the back of the plinth.*

WALSH (*with a certain levity*). *My* opinion, eh? I don't know why you need it. You've got *him*, haven't you? (*He waggles the skeleton's foot familiarly.*) What more d'you want? (*He comes forward and sits on the front of the plinth, looking at the other two* COLLIERS.) Aye, or you too, with your natty little nosegays dandled in your hatbands. Take 'em out, sharp! He's learnt you the truth, hasn't he?

They remove their cockades, shamefacedly.

PUGNACIOUS COLLIER. All right, *that'll* do.

WALSH. Will it, matey, will it? If it helps you to remember what we've been fighting for, I daresay it will. Trade Unions aren't formed, you know, so we can all have beer-ups on the Army.

SLOW COLLIER. He said that'll do. I'm sick and bloody tired – I don't know *what* it's all about.

WALSH (*drops down to the forestage*). Come home and I'll tell you. The circus is over. Come on.

MUSGRAVE. Oh no it's not. Just bide still a while. There's more to be said yet. When I asked you your opinion I meant about them we was talking about – them as did *this*, up here.

WALSH. Well, *what* about them – brother? Clear enough to me. You go for a soldier, you find yourself in someone else's country, you deserve all you get. *I'd* say it stands to reason.

MUSGRAVE. And that's *all* you would say? I'd thought better of you.

WALSH (*irritated*). Now look, look here, what *are* you trying to get? You come to this place all hollering for sympathy, oh you've been beating and murdering and following your trade boo-hoo: but we're not bloody interested! You mend your own heartache and leave us to sort with ours – we've enough and to spare!

MUSGRAVE (*very intensely*). This *is* for your heart. Take another look at *him*. (*Points to skeleton.*) Go on, man, both eyes, and carefully. Because you all used to know him: or most of you did. Private Billy Hicks, late of this parish, welcome him back from the wars, he's bronzed and he's fit, with many a tall tale of distant campaigning to spin round the fireside – ah, *you* used to know him, *didn't* you, Mrs. Hitchcock!

MRS. HITCHCOCK *has risen in great alarm.*

SLOW COLLIER. That's never Billy Hicks, ye dirty liar.

PUGNACIOUS COLLIER. He wor my putter for two year, when I hewed coal in number five – he hewed there hisself for nigh on a year alongside o' my brother.

SLOW COLLIER. He left his clogs to me when he went to join up – that's never our Billy.

NOISES OFF. Never Billy. Never Billy.

BARGEE. 'Never Billy Hicks' – 'Never Billy Hicks' – they don't dare believe it. You've knocked 'em to the root, boy. Oh the white faces!

MRS. HITCHCOCK. She ought to be told. She's got a right to know.

MUSGRAVE. Go along then and tell her.

HURST (*to* MUSGRAVE). You letting her go

MUSGRAVE. Yes.

HURST. But –

MUSGRAVE (*curtly*). Attend to your orders.

MRS. HITCHCOCK *goes out.*

When I say it's Billy Hicks, you can believe me it's true.

WALSH. Aye, I'll believe you. And you know what I think – it's downright indecent!

MUSGRAVE. Aye, aye? But wait. Because here is the reason. I'm a religious man, and I see the causes of the Almighty in every human work.

PARSON. That is absolute blasphemy!

MAYOR. This won't do you a pennorth o' good, you know.

MUSGRAVE. Not to me, no. But maybe to you? Now as I understand the workings of God, through greed and the world, this man didn't die because he went alone to the opera, he was killed because he had to be – it being decided; that now the people in that city was worked right up to killing soldiers, then more and more soldiers should be sent for them to kill, and the soldiers in turn should kill the people in that city, more and more, always – that's what I said to you: four men, one girl, then the twenty-five and the nine – *and* it'll go on, there or elsewhere, and it can't be stopped neither, except there's someone finds out Logic and brings the wheel round. You see, the Queen's Book, which eighteen years I've lived, it's turned inside out for *me*. There used to be my duty: now there's a disease –

HURST. Wild-wood mad.

MUSGRAVE. Wild-wood mad we are; and so we've fetched it home. You've had Moses and the Prophets – that's *him* – (*He points at* WALSH.) – 'cos he told you. But you were all for enlisting, it'd still have gone on. Moses and the Prophets, what good did they do?

He sits down and broods. There is a pause.

WALSH (*awkwardly*). There's no one from this town be over

keen to join up now. You've preached your little gospel: I daresay we can go home?

MUSGRAVE *makes no reply. The* SOLDIERS *look at one another doubtfully.*

HURST. What do we do now?

ATTERCLIFFE. Wait.

HURST. Serjeant –

ATTERCLIFFE (*shushing him*). Ssh-ssh!

A pause. Restive noises, off.

HURST. Serjeant –

ATTERCLIFFE. Serjeant – they've heard your message, they'll none of them forget it. Haven't we done what we came for?

HURST (*astonished, to* ATTERCLIFFE). Done what we came for?

ATTERCLIFFE *shushes him again as* MUSGRAVE *stirs.*

MUSGRAVE (*as though to himself*). One man, and for him five. Therefore, for five of them we multiply out, *and* we find it five-and-twenty. . . . So, as I understand Logic and Logic to me is the mechanism of God – that means that today there's twenty-five persons will have to be –

ATTERCLIFFE *jumps up in horror.* ANNIE *and* MRS. HITCHCOCK *appear at the upper window. When she sees the skeleton* ANNIE *gasps and seems about to scream.*

MUSGRAVE (*cutting her short*). It's true. It's him. You don't need to cry out; you knew it when he left you.

ANNIE. Take him down. Let me have him. I'll come down for him now.

BARGEE. Away down, me strong Annie. I'll carry you a golden staircase – aha, she's the royal champion, stand by as she comes down.

As he speaks he jumps on to the plinth, takes away the ladder, nips across the stage and props it under the window.

MUSGRAVE. No! Let her wait up there. I said: wait! . . . Now then, who's with me! Twenty-five to die and the Logic is worked out. Who'll help me? You? (*He points to* WALSH.) I made sure that you would: you're a man like the Black Musgrave, you: you have purposes, and you can lead. Join along with my madness, friend. I brought it back to England but I've brought the cure too – to turn it on to them that sent it out of this country – way-out-ay they sent it, where they hoped that only soldiers could catch it and rave! Well here's three redcoat ravers on their own kitchen hearthstone! Who do we start with? These? (*He turns on the* MAYOR.) 'Loyal hearts and true, every man jack of us.' (*To the* PARSON.) 'Draw the sword with gladness.' Why, *swords* is for honour, carry 'em on church parade, a *sword'll* never offer you three hundred and fifty bullets in a minute – and it was no bright sword neither finished *his* life in a back street! (*He points to* BILLY, *and then at the* CONSTABLE.) Or what about the Peeler? If we'd left it to *him*, *you'd* ha' been boxed away to barracks six or eight hours ago! Come on now, let's have you, you know I'm telling you truth!

WALSH. Nay: it won't do.

HURST. It won't do? Why not?

WALSH. I'm not over clear why not. Last night there was me and some others tried to whip away that Gatling. And we'd ha' used it and all: by God, there was need. But that's one thing, y'see, and this is another – ent it, you tell me?

He appeals to the COLLIERS.

PUGNACIOUS COLLIER. Nay, I don't know.

SLOW COLLIER. I think they're all balmy, the whole damn capful's arse-over-tip –

WALSH. No it's not. *I'm* not. And it comes to this wi' me: *he's* still in uniform, and he's still got his Book. He's doing his duty. Well, I take no duties from no bloody lobsters. This town lives by collieries. That's coal-owners and it's pitmen

– aye, and they battle, and the pitmen'll win. But not wi' no soldier-boys to order our fight for us. Remember their trade: you give 'em one smell of a broken town, you'll never get 'em out!

MUSGRAVE (*with growing desperation*). But you don't understand me – all of you, listen! I told you we could *cure* –

ATTERCLIFFE. I don't think you can.

MUSGRAVE (*flabbergasted*). Eh? What's that? Stay by your weapon!

ATTERCLIFFE. No. (*He stands away from the gun.*)

HURST *rapidly takes his place.*

HURST (*to the crowd*). Keep still, the lot of you!

ATTERCLIFFE. It won't do, Black Jack. You swore there'd be no killing.

MUSGRAVE. No I did not.

ATTERCLIFFE. You gave us to believe. We've done what we came for, and it's there we should have ended. *I've* ended. No killing.

He deliberately gets down from the platform, and squats on the ground. MUSGRAVE *looks around him, appealing and appalled.*

BARGEE. I'm with you, general!

MUSGRAVE. You?

BARGEE. Nobody else! I'll serve you a lovely gun! Rapine and riot! (*He scrambles on to the plinth, picks up a rifle from the box and loads it.*) When do we start breaking open the boozers? Or the pawnshops and all – who's for a loot?

MUSGRAVE. None of you at all? Come on, come on, why, he was your Billy, wasn't he? That you knew and you worked with – don't you want to revenge him?

ANNIE. Somebody hold the ladder. I'm going to come down.

The SLOW COLLIER *does so.*

MUSGRAVE (*urgently, to her*). Billy Hicks, lassie: here: he used to be yours! Tell them what they've got to do: tell them the truth!

ANNIE *has started to come down the ladder. When she is down, the* COLLIER *lowers it to the ground.*

HURST. Wait a minute, serjeant, leave me to talk to them! We've not got time bothering wi' no squalling tarts.

MUSGRAVE. Keep you your place.

HURST (*furiously*). I'm in my bloody place! And I'll tell you this straight, if we lose this crowd now, we've lost all the work, for ever! And remember summat else. There's Dragoons on the road!

General sensation. Shouts off: 'Dragoons'.

HURST (*to the crowd*). So you've just got five minutes to make up your minds.

He grabs his rifle up, and motions the BARGEE *violently to the Gatling. The* BARGEE *takes over, and* HURST *leaps off the plinth and talks straight into the* COLLIERS' *faces and at the audience.*

We've earned our living by beating and killing folk like yourselves in the streets of their own city. Well, it's drove us mad – and so we come back here to tell you how and to show you what it's like. The ones we want to deal with aren't, for a change, you and your mates, but a bit higher up. The ones as never get hurt. (*He points at the* MAYOR, PARSON *and* CONSTABLE.) Him. Him. Him. You hurt them hard, and they'll not hurt you again. And they'll not send *us* to hurt you neither. But if you let 'em be, then us three'll be killed – aye and worse, we'll be forgotten – and the whole bloody lot'll start all over again!

He climbs back and takes over the gun.

MUSGRAVE. For God's sake stand with us. We've *got* to be remembered!

SLOW COLLIER. We ought to, you know. He might be right.

WALSH. I don't know. I don't trust it.

PUGNACIOUS COLLIER. Ahr and be damned, these are just like the same as us. Why don't we stand with 'em?

WALSH (*obstinately*). I've not yet got this clear.

ANNIE. To me it's quite clear. He asked me to tell you the truth. My truth's an easy tale, it's old true-love gone twisted, like they called it 'malformed'– they put part in the ground, and hang the rest on a pillar here, and expect me to sit under it making up song-ballads. All right.

> My true love is a scarecrow
> Of rotted rag and bone
> Ask him : where are the birds, Billy?
> Where have they all gone?

He says: Unbutton my jacket, and they'll all fly out of the ribs – oh, oh, I'm not mad, though you told us that *you* were – let's have that bundle!

MRS. HITCHCOCK *throws down a bundle.* ANNIE *shakes it out, revealing* SPARKY'S *tunic.*

Take a sight o' this, you hearty colliers : see what they've brought you. You can match it up with Billy's. Last night there were four o' these walking, weren't there? Well, this morning there's three. They buried the other one in Ma Hitchcock's midden. Go on, ask 'em why!

HURST. He's a deserter, is why!

ANNIE (*holding up the tunic*). Hey, here's the little hole where they let in the bayonet. Eee, aie, easily in. His blood's on my tongue, so hear what it says. A bayonet is a raven's beak. This tunic's a collier's jacket. That scarecrow's a birdcage. What more do you want!

WALSH. Is this what she says true? Where *is* he, the fourth of you?

MUSGRAVE. He was killed, and that's all. By an accident killed. It's barely materi –

ATTERCLIFFE. Oh, it's material. And no goddamned accident. I said it to you, Musgrave, it washes it all out.

WALSH. It bloody does and all, as far as I go. (*He turns to the other* COLLIERS.) If you want to stand by 'em when they've done for their own mucker and not one of the bastards can tell ye the same tale, well, you're at your damned liberty and take it and go!

The COLLIERS *murmur dubiously.*

HURST (*frantic*). I'm going to start shooting!

General reaction of fear: he clearly means it. He spits at MUSGRAVE.

You and your everlasting Word – you've pulled your own roof down! But *I'll* prop your timber for you – I'll give a One, Two, and a Three: and I'm opening fire!

ATTERCLIFFE. No.

He jumps up and stands on the step of the plinth, below the gun and facing it, with his arms spread out so that the muzzle is against his breast.

HURST (*distorted with rage*). Get down! Get down off it, you old cuckold, I don't care who you are. I'll put the first one *through* you! I *swear* it, I will! One! Two! . . .

MAYOR (*to the* CONSTABLE). Go for that gun.

The CONSTABLE *is making a cautious move towards the gun, but he is forestalled by* MUSGRAVE, *who flings himself at* HURST *and knocks him away from the breach. There is a moment's tense struggle behind the gun.*

MUSGRAVE (*as he struggles*). The wrong way. The wrong way. You're trying to do it without Logic.

Then HURST *gives way and falls back down the steps of the plinth. He recovers himself.*

HURST (*panting with excitement*). All right then, Black Jack. All right, it's finished. The lot. You've lost it. I'm off!

MUSGRAVE (*stunned*). Come back here. You'll come back, you'll obey orders.

HURST *makes a grab forward, snatches his rifle from the platform and jumps back clear.*

HURST (*to the crowd*). Get out o' my road!

At the very instant he turns towards the wings to run away, a shot is fired offstage. His quick turn changes into a grotesque leap as the bullet hits him, and he collapses on the stage. A bugle blares from offstage.

VOICES OFF. Dragoons!

Orders shouted and general noise of cavalry coming to a halt and dismounting.

MAYOR } (*one after another, rapidly.*)
CONSTABLE } The Dragoons! The Dragoons!
PARSON } Saved! Saved! Saved!

VOICES OFF. Saved! Saved! Saved!

MUSGRAVE *is standing beside the gun, temporarily at a loss.* ATTERCLIFFE *has jumped down beside* HURST *and lifted his head. Everyone else stands amazed.*
Suddenly MUSGRAVE *swings the gun to point toward the Dragoons. The* BARGEE *ups with his rifle and sticks it into* MUSGRAVE'S back.

BARGEE. Serjeant, put your hands up!

MUSGRAVE *is pushed forward by the rifle, but he does not obey. The* TROOPER *enters, clicking the bolt of his smoking carbine, and shouting.*

TROOPER. Everybody stand where you are! You, put your hands up!

MUSGRAVE *does so.*

BARGEE. I've got him, soldier! I've got him! Crooked Joe's got him, Mr. Mayor.

The OFFICER *strides in, drawing his sabre.*

Give a cheer – hooroar!

Cheers off.
The OFFICER *comes to attention before the* MAYOR *and salutes with his sabre.*

OFFICER. Mr. Mayor, are we in time?
MAYOR. Aye, you're in time. You're *just* in bloody time.
OFFICER (*seeing* MUSGRAVE). 22128480 Serjeant Musgrave, J.?
MUSGRAVE. My name.
OFFICER. We heard word you'd come here. You are under arrest. Robbery and desertion. There were *three* who came with you.
ATTERCLIFFE (*getting up from* HURST, *whose head falls back.*) You can count me for one of them. One other's dead already. Here's the third.
OFFICER. You're under arrest.
CONSTABLE. Hold out your hands.

He takes out two pairs of handcuffs and fetters them.

OFFICER. Mr. Mayor, my troopers are at your disposal. What do you require of us?
MAYOR. Well, I'd say it was about all over by now, young man – wouldn't you?
OFFICER. Law and order is established?
PARSON. Wiser counsels have prevailed, Captain.
BARGEE. *I* caught him, *I* caught him, *I* used me strategy!

OFFICER. My congratulations, all.

WALSH (*with great bitterness*). The community's been saved. Peace and prosperity rules. We're all friends and neighbours for the rest of today. We're all sorted out. We're back where we were. So what do we do?

BARGEE.

Free beer. It's still here.
No more thinking. Easy drinking.
End of a bad bad dream. Gush forth the foaming stream.

He takes the bung out of the barrel and starts filling tankards.

OFFICER. The winter's broken up. Let normal life begin again.

BARGEE. Aye, aye, *begin* again!

He is handing the mugs to the people. He starts singing, and they all join in, by degrees.

There was an old man called Michael Finnegan
He had whiskers on his chin-egan
The wind came out and blew them in agen
Poor old Michael Finnegan –
Begin agen –

There was an old man etcetera . . .

He gives out mugs in the following order: the MAYOR, *the* PARSON, *the* SLOW COLLIER, *the* PUGNACIOUS COLLIER, *the* CONSTABLE. *Each man takes his drink, swigs a large gulp, then links wrists with the previous one, until all are dancing round the centre-piece in a chain, singing.*

ANNIE *has climbed the plinth and lowers the skeleton. She sits with it on her knees. The* DRAGOONS *remain standing at the side of the stage.* MUSGRAVE *and* ATTERCLIFFE *come slowly downstage. The* BARGEE *fills the last two tankards and hands one to* WALSH, *who turns his back angrily. The* BARGEE *empties one mug, and joins the tail of the dance, still holding the*

other. After one more round he again beckons WALSH. *This time the latter thinks for a moment, then bitterly throws his hat on the ground, snarls into the impassive face of the* DRAGOON, *and joins in the dance, taking the beer.*
The scene closes, leaving MUSGRAVE *and* ATTERCLIFFE *on the forestage.* MRS. HITCHCOCK *retires from the window.*

SCENE TWO

A prison cell.

This scene is achieved by a barred wall descending in front of the dancers of the previous scene. After a while the sound dies away, and the lights change so that we can no longer see past the bars. MUSGRAVE *remains standing, looking into the distance with his back to the audience.* ATTERCLIFFE *sighs and sits down gingerly on the floor.*

ATTERCLIFFE. Sit down and rest yourself, serjeant. That's all there is left . . . Go on, man, sit down . . . Then stand and the devil take you! It's *your* legs, not mine. It's my *hands* is what matters. They finished Sparky and that finished me, and Sparky finished you. Holy God save us, why warn't I a greengrocer, then I'd never ha' been cuckolded, never gone for no soldier, never no dead Sparky, and never none of this. Go on, serjeant, talk to me. I'm an old old stupid bastard and I've nowt to do now but fret out the runs of the consequence; and the whole croaking work it's finished and done. Go on, serjeant, talk.

MUSGRAVE *does not move.*
A pause.
MRS. HITCHCOCK *enters, carrying a glass.*

MRS. HITCHCOCK (*to* MUSGRAVE). It's port with a bit o'

lemon. I often take it of a morning; like it settles me stummick for the day. The officer said I could see you, if I warn't no more nor five minutes. Sit down and I'll give it to your mouth – them wrist-irons makes it difficult, I daresay.

MUSGRAVE (*without looking at her*). Give it to him. I don't want it.

MRS. HITCHCOCK. He can have half of it. You take a sup first.

MUSGRAVE *shakes his head.*

All right. How you like.

She goes to ATTERCLIFFE *and puts the glass to his mouth.*

ATTERCLIFFE. I'm obliged to you, missus.

MRS. HITCHCOCK. It's on the house, this one. Change from the Queen, ent it?

MUSGRAVE. Numbers and order. According to Logic. I had worked it out for months.

He swings round to MRS. HITCHCOCK.

What made it break down!

MRS. HITCHCOCK. Ah, there's the moral of it. You ask our Annie.

MUSGRAVE (*furiously*). He was killed by pure accident! It had nothing to do –

ATTERCLIFFE. Oh by God, it had.

MRS. HITCHCOCK. The noisy one, warn't he? Pack o' cards and all the patter. You asked me to trust you – (*her voice rises with rage and emotion*) – he was only a young lad, for gracious goodness Christ, he'd a voice like a sawmill – what did you want to do it for, you gormless great gawk!

ATTERCLIFFE. *He* didn't do it.

MRS. HITCHCOCK. He did, oh he did! And he broke his own neck.

MUSGRAVE. What's the matter with you, woman!

MRS. HITCHCOCK. All wrong, you poured it out all wrong! I

could ha' told you last night if only I'd known – the end of the world and you thought you could call a parade. In control – *you!*

MUSGRAVE (*very agitated*). Don't talk like that. You're talking about my duty. Good order and the discipline: it's the only road I know. Why can't you see it?

MRS. HITCHCOCK. All I can see is Crooked Joe Bludgeon having his dance out in the middle of fifty Dragoons! It's time you learnt your life, you big proud serjeant. Listen: last evening you told all about this anarchy and where it came from – like, scribble all over with life or love, and that makes anarchy. Right?

MUSGRAVE. Go on.

MRS. HITCHCOCK. Then *use* your Logic – if you can. Look at it this road: here we are, and we'd got life and love. Then *you* came in and you did your scribbling where nobody asked you. Aye, it's arsy-versey to what you said, but it's still an anarchy, isn't it? And it's all your work.

MUSGRAVE. Don't tell me there was life or love in this town.

MRS. HITCHCOCK. There was. There was hungry men, too – fighting for their food. But *you* brought in a different war.

MUSGRAVE. I brought it in to end it.

ATTERCLIFFE. To end it by its own rules: no bloody good. She's right, you're wrong. You can't cure the pox by further whoring. Sparky died of those damned rules. And so did the other one.

MUSGRAVE. That's not the truth. (*He looks at them both in appeal, but they nod.*) That's not the truth. God was with me . . . God . . . (*He makes a strange animal noise of despair, a sort of sob that is choked off suddenly, before it can develop into a full howl.*) – and all they dancing – all of them – there.

MRS. HITCHCOCK. Ah, not for long. And it's not a dance of joy. Those men are hungry, so they've got no time for *you*. One day they'll be full, though, and the Dragoons'll be gone, and then they'll remember.

MUSGRAVE (*shaking his head*). No.

MRS. HITCHCOCK. Let's hope it, any road, Eh?

She presents the glass to his lips. This time he accepts it and drinks, and remains silent.

ATTERCLIFFE (*melancholy but quiet*). That running tyke of a Sparky, he reckoned he wor the only bastard in the barracks had a voice. Well, he warn't. There's other men can sing when he's not here. So listen at this.

He sings.

I plucked a blood-red rose-flower down
And gave it to my dear.
I set my foot out across the sea
And she never wept a tear.

I came back home as gay as a bird
I sought her out and in:
And I found her at last in a little attic room
With a napkin round her chin.

At her dinner, you see. Very neat and convenient.

He sings.

Oh are you eating meat, I said,
Or are you eating fish?
I'm eating an apple was given me today,
The sweetest I could wish.

So I asked her where she got it, and by God the tune changed then. Listen at what she told me.

He sings to a more heavily accented version of the tune.

Your blood-red rose is withered and gone
And fallen on the floor:
And he who brought the apple down
Shall be my darling dear.

For the apple holds a seed will grow
In live and lengthy joy
To raise a flourishing tree of fruit
For ever and a day.
With fal-la-la-the-dee, toor-a-ley,
For ever and a day.

They're going to hang us up a length higher nor most apple-trees grow, Serjeant. D'you reckon we can start an orchard?

Notes

(These notes are intended for use by overseas students as well as by English-born readers.)

Act One

9 *WD broad arrow* – War Department, which had a broad arrow as its sign.
9 *recruiting party* – group of soldiers whose task is to get men to join the army.
9 *enlisted* – formally taken into the army.
9 *attested* – put on oath as a soldier.
9 *Royal Barracks* – large building for lodging soldiers
9 *Crimea* – area of southern Russia, where the Crimean War (1854-6) took place, great hardship being suffered during the Russian winter.
9 *field kitchens* – kitchens of an army encampment.
9 *Sebastopol* – a town lengthily besieged during the Crimean War.
9 *provost-sarnt* – a provost sergeant was a sergeant in the military police.
9 *corporal-cook* – a corporal in charge of cooking.
9 *Commissary* – officer in charge of the commissariat or food and stores.
9 *Regiment* – the largest sub-division of the British army, consisting of several battalions.
9 *agen* – again.
10 *bugle and drum* – used as signals for doing anything in the army.
10 *serjeant* – old fashioned spelling of sergeant.
10 *court martial* – trial of a soldier by officers for an offence against military law.
10 *blockhouse* – detached fort.
10 *any road* – anyway.
11 *'Michael Finnegan'* – cyclical song in which the same verse is repeated over and over again: see p.99.
11 *my jolly buckos* – good fellows.

11 *barge* – flat bottomed boat which conveys goods and sometimes people along canals.
11 *old horse* – a barge was towed by a horse walking along the canal bank.
12 *mucker* – mate, comrade, friend.
12 *Gatling gun* – early kind of automatic gun, a fore-runner of the machine gun.
12 *cat-o'-nine-tails* – many-thonged whip.
12 *wor* – was (north-of-England dialect).
13 *fast* – firmly closed, impassable.
13 *recruities* – recruits.
13 *conies* – old word for rabbits. Coney-catcher was a slang term for a cheater of credulous or foolish victims.
14 *Queen* – at this period, Queen Victoria – often referred to in the play as if she were the personal employer of the country's army.
14 *not material* – not relevant or important (Musgrave's characteristic comment).
14 *Empire* – Queen Victoria took the title of Queen Empress in 1876 in recognition of her dominion over India and various other countries; reference to the 'British Empire' became usual after this.
14 *nowt* – nothing (north-of-England dialect).
14 *Parson* – commonly used of any clergyman of the Church of England.
14 *licence* – public houses need a licence permitting them to sell alcoholic drinks.
14 *magistrate* – citizen who has the civil office of administering law, especially minor offences.
15 *agen* – against (dialect).
15 *Bench* – magistrate's or judge's official seat; used as short name for the office of being a magistrate or judge.
15 *going on the parish* – having to take money from the parish, an area having its own parish church, responsible for certain very local affairs including payments to the poor.
15 *workhouse* – institution set up in a parish to house destitute people, where they had to work as long as they remained.
15 *arsy-versy* – topsy-turvy, upside down.
15 *crossroads* – in a mistaken or hostile way.
15 *His Worship the Mayor* – head of the civic authorities of a town.
15 *scarlet* – a mayor's robes can be scarlet.
16 *taddy* – beer brewed in Tadcaster, well known in Northern England.

17 *tests it* – false coin of bad metal would bend
19 *stand by your beds* – a common army command, not appropriate here.
19 *doss down* – sleep on a makeshift bed.
19 *chalk it up* – money owed is chalked up on a slate to be paid later.
19 *coach-house* – building for horse-drawn coaches.
19 *bayonet* – stabbing blade attached to a rifle.
19 *Queen as pays* – payment will be made later from official army funds.
20 *Constable* – member of the police force.
21 *gold chain* – a mayor's badge of office.
21 *snug* – small drinking room, usually cosy and comfortable.
22 *has fell/cut me wages* – instead of the correct 'has fallen/cut my wages'; the Mayor's ungrammatical speech shows he has become rich only after an uneducated and probably poor childhood.
22 *summat* – something (dialect).
22 *Royal Shilling* – one shilling was paid to confirm that a recruit had joined the army.
22 *deputy-specials* – ordinary untrained citizens, acting as temporary assistants to the police.
23 *Council* – the town council administers local civic affairs.
23 *every man-jack* – each one.
23 *flock to the colours* – hurry in crowds to join the army.
23 *golden sovereign* – gold coin worth one pound.
23 *set* – sit (dialect).
23 *fannies* – bottoms, buttocks.
23 *owt* – anything (dialect).
23 *reconnaissance* – military term for a survey of an area.
24 *nattering* – chattering, gossiping.
25 *off-handed* – casually, without interest.
26 *daft* – crazy, mentally defective.
26 *pissed* – drunk.
29 *Company* – sub-division of an infantry battalion.
29 *what the time is* – i.e. give me orders unnecessarily.
30 *orderly room* – the office and court of a commanding officer.
30 *three stripes* – worn on the sleeve indicating the rank of sergeant.
30 *State of Emergency* – when normal laws are suspended by the government so that rapid (usually military) action can be taken.

30 *high standard of turnout, military bearing* – good equipment and uniform and appearance, demanded of soldiers at all times.
30 *civvy* – civilian.
31 *lugs* – ears.
31 *pick hefts* – pickaxe handles.
32 *clogs* – wooden or wooden-soled shoes, worn by the poor in the north of England at this period.
32 *lobster* – soldier; boiled lobster is red like the soldiers' tunics.
34 *Absent. Not sober. Improperly dressed* – military offences.
35 *squad* – small number or party of soldiers.
36 *wild-wood mad* – wild-wood: untamed woodland; perhaps the sense is: as mad as a wild man of the woods.
36 *A Pillar of Flame* – God guided the Israelites to safety appearing as a pillar of flame by night (Exodus xiii 21). This speech is full of Biblical references.

Act Two

38 *empties* – empty glasses or bottles.
38 *well-oiled* – fairly drunk.
38 *platoon* – subdivision of an infantry company.
38 *dress the ranks* – take up position exactly aligned in rows.
39 *drill* – perform military exercises, particularly marching in formation on the parade ground.
39 *muster* – assemble in formation for inspection.
39 *billets* – citizen's houses where soldiers are forcibly lodged.
40 *lark* – game, trick.
41 *Backwards-Mounted-Foot/Queen's Own Randy Chancers, etc.* – nonsense names of imaginary regiments.
42 *Queen o' Spades* – supposed to foretell bad luck (see Commentary p. xxviii.
42 *an Englishman, a Welshman* – many jokes begin in this way, basing their point on supposed differences between the nationalities.
42 *on Defaulters* – being punished for a military offence.
42 *Hoots awa'* – supposed to be a typical Scottish exclamation.
44 *lady-killing* – expecting to impress women.
44 *between me porridge and me bacon* – between the usual first and second courses of breakfast.
45 *Time, gentlemen please* – time, gentlemen please is the traditional call of the publican at closing time.
46 *closhy* – closh is an unusual name for a cattle disease but here 'closhy' is probably a made-up word suggesting something unpleasant.

47 *peeler* – Policeman, named after Sir Robert Peel, popularly regarded as founder of the police force.
48 *curfew* – prohibition of being in the streets after a certain hour.
48 *hotel-resident* – residents staying in a hotel are legally permitted to drink outside the usual hours.
48 *By Appointment* – suppliers of goods to the Royal Household are sometimes allowed to write 'By Appointment' on signs and advertisements.
48 *Windsor Castle* – a main residence of the Queen.
48 *Coldstream* – members of the Coldstream Guards, one of the four regiments of foot guards.
50 *loose-box* – stall in which a horse can move about.
50 *Yes-sarnt-no-sarnt, etc . . .* – a children's rhyme *Baa Baa Black Sheep* has the lines 'Yes Sir, no Sir, three bags full'; generally quoted to imply mock servility.
50 *Oaks, Derby* – names of famous, regularly-held horse races.
50 *steeple-chase* – horse race across country or a course, which includes jumps over hedges or other obstacles.
50 *pressgangs* – bodies employed to force unwilling men to join the navy (or, here, the army).
52 *To bed to bed etc. . .* – children's rhyme, the last two lines of which usually read 'Put on the pan, says greedy Nan,
Let's sup before we go'.
52 *'Fred Karno'* – the author is referring to the turn-of-the-century music-hall comedian, who by the First World War had become synonymous with anything farcical and absurd.
53 *To the front present* – an order to soldiers to hold their firearms in a formal position in front of the body.
53 *Order arms* – an order to hold the firearm against the right side of the body with its butt on the ground.
53 *on the spot* – at once.
53 *Old-Mother-Bunch* – noted London ale seller of the late 16th century.
53 *Popshop* – pawnbroker's shop, where goods are left as security for borrowing money.
53 *guineas* – coins worth one pound, one shilling.
54 *ninepins* – wooden pegs or skittles, to be knocked down in a ball game.
57 *gab* – chatter, talk.
57 *tart* – prostitute.
57 *'reveille'* – bugle call, signal for waking.
59 *capped* – finished.

62 *gobs* – mouths.
63 *clover* – its leaf has three lobes on one stalk.
64 *Fire, fire/London's Burning* – lines from a song about the Great Fire of London, 1666.
65 *poorly* – ill.
66 *grog* – drink of spirits, especially rum and water.
65 *right-marker* – soldier at the right end of a row, by which all the others align themselves.
66 *boozer* – public house.
69 *midden* – heap of muck, manure.
72 *nignog* – fool (19th-century army slang).
74 *bully* – good fellow.
74 *Dragoons* – cavalrymen of certain regiments.

Act Three

76 *practicable* – can be used, not just painted on cardboard.
76 *fugleman* – leader or guide to a crowd; originally a soldier set out as a model or example.
77 *Hark, hark* – a children's rhyme, which really runs
Hark, hark, the dogs do bark
The beggars are coming to town
Some in rags and some in jags
And one in a velvet gown
77 *real live* – typical showman's praise for such sights as circus animals or freaks – obviously not appropriate to ale or sovereigns.
77 *previous* – premature.
78 *'taters* – potatoes (dialect).
78 *straight from the shoulder* – direct, like a straight blow in boxing.
78 *pulls no punches* – to pull a punch is to hold back while pretending to punch, as in a corrupt boxing match.
79 *Rector* – parson.
79 *'And Jesus said' etc.* – Matthew IX xxxiv
79 *in the name of the Father, etc.* – 'In the name of the Father, and of the Son and of the Holy Ghost, Amen' is the usual conclusion of a blessing in the Church of England service.
81 *RSM* – Regimental Sergeant Major.
81 *bull* – undue insistence on the smart appearance of dress or equipment.
81 *squaddy* – ordinary soldier, member of a squad.
83 *Union Jack* – national flag of Great Britain.
84 *Last Post* – Last bugle call before lights out, also played at military funerals.

85 *balmy* – silly, insane.
86 *Protectorate* – state which is controlled by a stronger one.
86 *WOL* – without leave, without permission.
88 *off his nut* – mad, crazy.
88 *beer-ups* – drinking sessions.
89 *hollering* – shouting.
89 *bronzed and he's fit* – terms of admiration often used to praise soldiers and army life.
89 *putter* – man or boy who pushed the barrows of coal along in a mine.
92 *whip away* – steal.
92 *capful* – lot.
92 *arse over tip* – upside down, totally confused.
95 *Ma Hitchcock* – Mother Hitchcock
99 *swigs* – drinks.
101 *stummick* – stomach (dialect).
101 *on the house* – free.
101 *gormless* – stupid.
101 *gawk* – awkward person.
102 *pox* – venereal disease.
103 *tyke* – dog.

Hurst, Musgrave and Bargee at the market cross in the 1959 production (*Photo: Snowdon*)

The Parson, the Constable and the Mayor (*above*) and the churchyard scene (*below*) from the 1965 revival (*Photos: Dominic*)